Vital Signs

POEMS OF ILLNESS AND HEALING

Vital Signs

POEMS OF ILLNESS AND HEALING

EDITED BY MARTIN DYAR

Poetry
Ireland
Éigse
Éireann

For Gillian

Poetry Ireland CLG / Éigse Éireann CTR gratefully acknowledges the assistance of The Arts Council / An Chomhairle Ealaíon and The Arts Council of Northern Ireland.

Poetry Ireland invites individuals and commercial organisations to become Patrons of Poetry Ireland.
For more details, please contact:
Anne Hendrick,
Development Manager,
Poetry Ireland, 11 Parnell Square East,
Dublin 1, Ireland
Telephone +353 1 6789815; e-mail development@poetryireland.ie

ISBN: 978-1-902121-90-1

Project Manager: **Kerrie O'Brien**

Publications Manager: **Paul Lenehan**, with **Molly O'Toole**

Cover design and illustrations by **Rob Torrans**
www.robtorrans.com

First published by Poetry Ireland, 2022
www.poetryireland.ie

CONTENTS

Foreword

The misconception still exists, in some corners of this modern age, that science and the arts occupy two distinct and separate spaces, that indeed as interests or aptitudes they could not be more dissimilar. Thankfully, this fallacy is fading; and in this remarkable anthology it is movingly and eloquently challenged.

We are brought in diverse ways to a juncture in which the relationship of perpetual exchange that is shared between science and creativity is at, perhaps, its most vital, the recognition and experience of vulnerability. While the work in this anthology reminds us that medical advances have played an important role in the revitalising experience that death can become, it simultaneously speaks of the inherent complexity of intimacy and longing in the human being, and the great imagination required to balance and navigate that intricate humanity, within the self and with others. In so much of this the necessity for, but also the insufficiency of, the rational has to be recognised and respected.

Walter Isaacson has said that 'science gives us the empirical data and the theories to tie them together, but humans turn them into narratives with moral, emotional and historical meaning.' The poems brought together in this publication provide such an act of balancing, offering as they do an all-encompassing view of the experience of illness, medical intervention, and death in our lives. They invite us to enter into the circumstance of that world that none of us can avoid indefinitely or transact adequately through the prisms of individual narratives, into those final days of a life during which every event and every hour in its recovery beyond the self enables a transcendence that can so often be a singular and heightened experience.

Dennis O'Driscoll for example exclaims:

> recall how glorious it seemed,
> your unwillingness to let go ...

While James Dickey in turn recalls his father:

> In the shape of his death still living.

Albert Einstein, that great unifier of reason and intuition, method and reflection, has said that:

> Imagination is more important than knowledge. For knowledge is limited to all we know and understand, while imagination embraces the entire world, and all there ever will be to know and understand.

Imagination contains within it the form of absent possibilities not realised but important in the task of recall. Einstein's words carry a salutary resonance in today's world where so many of our research institutions have come under pressure to focus on short-term outcomes and that which is measurable, basing their scientific, personal, and institutional reputation on what can be immediately quantifiable. Such a focus compromises that essential room for the independent thinking, courageous questioning, compassionate curiosity, and indeed the serendipitous findings which are so profoundly important to the practice of research and the formation of researchers.

It is the possibilities of an unknown future that drives the scientist and the researcher as powerfully as it does too the writers picking up their pen and beginning to draft a new poem, a new story, a new ending. Beyond preparation, an unconditional hospitality for the unpredictable visiting of the muse is important.

The reciprocal relationship between science and creativity is not a new or radical concept. Indeed, there was a time when art and science had not yet developed into distinct fields, the laboratory and the artist's or writer's studio both being understood as spaces of wondrous exploration. Both make it possible that new stories can begin. Those first steps are taken too towards unknown destinations where new ideas are fostered, and questions, whose answers are not yet known, are posed.

The work in this anthology makes a reflection, not only on the process of dying, but on the process of living in a world shaded by light and dark; what it means to be the medic:

Taking, giving back their lives,
By the strength of our bare hands,
By the silence of our knives …

Or to be the adult remembering how, as a child he was: 'the one who raced / down the roads to the far side of the town, / to the house by the river', to fetch the local doctor when someone had been injured. Or to be the patient who discovers, on leaving hospital, that:

> The world beyond the window
> was no vaster
> than the world inside the room ...

The powerful yet vulnerable humanity at the heart of each piece allows for a transcendence across the boundaries that so often falsely divide science from the arts or us, as persons, from each other. The works enable us to understand what it means to experience being fully human in all its complexity, fragility, and diversity.

In recent difficult times it was to both our scientists and our poets that we turned in search of hope and reassurance. As we anxiously watched the race to discover a vaccination against Covid 19, we also found solace in poems old and new, poems that suggested endurance and the light of resilience. In this anthology, Eiléan Ní Chuilleanáin's 'The Polio Epidemic' tells of how:

> The city lay empty, infected.
> There was no more ice-cream.
> The baths were closed all summer.

She was, of course, speaking of a different time, a different epidemic, a different country. But in her words we see, reflected, our own contemporary moment in all its challenges and new discoveries.

That constant rebirth of experience, bringing its perpetual seeking for new solutions, defines both the artistic and scientific dimensions of our shared lives. We are fortunate not to be in any forced circumstance of silence or shame, as was in the case of the misnamed Spanish flu of 1918. We have the privileged and emancipatory gift of words for the sharing.

In this anthology we read of life coming into the world and leaving it. We read of sudden moments of joy and delirium, of regrets encountered too late, of loss and love and fear and hope, of healing and death, of nature and science.

I am greatly honoured that one of my own poems, 'The Well 2', has been included in *Vital Signs*, a book that speaks of the world in all of its possibilities and all its wonderment and its sadness. This anthology brings us so deeply into that shared space in which we are constantly coming and going, arriving and departing, migrants in time and space.

Michael D. Higgins
Uachtarán na hÉireann
President of Ireland

Introduction

In the voyage of reading that led to the gathering of the contents of this anthology, I tried to let myself be guided by the quality and the implications of the poems themselves. Each poem included here has in some way influenced *Vital Signs* as a whole.

As the book progressed, I became accustomed to the delight of encountering a poem that seemed suitable, and to the ways that a new find could prompt a sense of adjustment, and even a sense of risk. Poems that struck me as excellent, poems I wanted to share, poems with an apparent glow of anthologisability, often suggested new aesthetic standards. They also tended to offer fresh ways of understanding the words 'illness' and 'healing', presenting in turn new possibilities for the purposes and scope of the work.

As much as it is concerned to enter a lesser-known poetic domain by discovering what poets have written in response to the human experience of illness and healing, and more broadly in response to the institutions of medicine and healthcare, *Vital Signs* is also intended more straightforwardly to be a book of poems. As such it can be read solely for the power and the interest of the writing. And that is one basic sense of its title: vitality in words.

Three centuries of poetry are represented. Robert Burns is the earliest writer, and there is a small number of poems chosen from books published in the past three years. There are two excerpted pieces, by Walt Whitman and Julie O'Callaghan. With both of these I have attempted to avoid a feeling of truncation, but the original texts are recommended to the reader. There are three long poems, by Dermot Healy, Seamus Heaney, and Anne Kennedy, which are included in full. There is also a selection in Irish, with accompanying translations.

I have chosen from Irish, UK, and American poetry, with a double bias towards poems from recent decades and poets writing in Ireland. I am grateful to Poetry Ireland, the publisher, for this liberty. In addition to re-moving ordinary geographic and historic boundaries and allowing impressions of difference and similarity, change and continuity to emerge, I have been able to position contemporary Irish poems in what seems a natural con-versation with poems from other territories and traditions, and with poems that are recognised as classics.

If this freedom has been an indulgence for the editor, I am confident that the result will not be disorienting for the living poets included. I am hopeful too that it amounts to a gift to the reader to have a universal subject explored in international and diverse terms within an avowedly Irish book. The opportunity to sample the rich-ness and promise of more recent poetry through its seem-ing ability to stand beside writing that has stood the test of time should be an intriguing one. And this prompts another angle for the book's title: here are hopeful signs of cultural life, and signs of the enduring good health of an ancient art form.

Vital Signs is arranged in five sections. For the sake of a fuller reading experience, to make room for serendipitous finds, and as a way of respecting the multiple intentions of the poets, I have not titled the sections according to their most relevant or obvious contents. Instead, each begins with an unattributed gateway quotation, which will be met again in its original home among the poetry that follows.

The poems have nonetheless been grouped together, and their complementary relationships are intended to be experienced as part of an over-arching structure, through which I have tried to establish a sense of illuminating pairings and development. Metaphorically speaking, there are discrete chapters and narratives at play. But at the same time these are not intended to distract from the sovereign voices of the poems.

In the first section there are poems set in (or which make reference to) hospitals, together with poems which consider healthcare professionals at work or in training. The intermingling of these two categories is intended as a way of populating the vividly drawn clinical worlds and patient circumstances with a series of professional or healer presences. Similarly, poems which might be said to give close consideration to medical ethics are glossed and extended by versions of the kinds of settings where healthcare work most often takes place. The anthology begins with Patrick Kavanagh's ironic statement, 'A year ago I fell in love with the functional ward / Of a chest hospital'. That poem presents a proud picture of acceptance in the face of chronic illness, and arrives at an instructive tone: 'For we must record love's mystery without claptrap'. In the final poem in the book, 'After Adomnán' by Tom French, the word 'must' appears again, in a refusal of despair that could serve as a *Vital Signs* hallmark:

"Those who have loved us and whom we have loved
must be permitted, at the very least,
to show each other what this life has meant."

The second section combines three interrelated sequences
of poems, beginning with the perspectives of family
members and friends who find themselves in the role of
carer or visitor to a sick person. Writing about adult
loved ones leads on to writing that is concerned with the
vulnerability of little ones, with a sample of what might
be called paediatric poems, a number of which recon-
struct the worlds of obstetrics and midwifery. The second
section concludes with a series of poems on public health
and pandemic related themes, where again love and
childhood are prominent.

This section concludes with Derek Mahon's 'Everything is Going to Be All Right'. Although without explicit
public health content, in recent years this poem became
for many people a quintessential coronavirus poem. The
appeal relates to Mahon's timely suggestion of a will
to face death without fear, and his holding fast to the
mysteries and consolations of poetry: 'The lines flow
from the hand unbidden / and the hidden source is the
watchful heart'. There is also the closing line's chorus-like
repetition of the poem's title, which denies the reality
of suffering, a riddle which, for all its unreasonableness,
conveys a relatable sense of courage.

What follows is intended as a response to Mahon's
comforting exhortation, which I have positioned as a kind
of midpoint. In some respects I have sought to put
pressure on the idea of a smooth and stoical resolution.
The poems at the beginning of the third section are

concerned with major and urgent problems. The forces of climate change and mainstream agriculture are evoked as matters of planetary health. The tragedies of homophobic violence are considered in the light of the idea of community wellbeing and the task of maintaining solidarity. There is also here a set of poems on war and conflict, which includes the surgeon in Miroslav Holub's 'Casualty' who blends a vision of medical altruism with a vision of the amorality of military interests.

The treatment of conflict is partnered with poems that question the authority and intentions of doctors, the equity and humanity of healthcare systems, and the effects of poverty and displacement on health. Here, as elsewhere, the neglect and abuse of women comes through with a passionate conviction and with anger. Hannah Copley's 'An Archive', Nandi Jola's 'Brussels (Will Fix Me)' and Celia de Fréine's 'Cailís mo Chuid Fola' (translated into English by the poet as 'Chalice of my Blood'), all work with a consciousness of inhumanity, and connect forward to the satirically framed knowledge of patriarchy contained in Shirley McClure's 'The Argument for Chemotherapy', which itself can be read as a probing of the significance of social class in doctor-patient relationships.

The main body of the third section combines poems which consider symptoms of illness in heightened terms. Pregnancy is featured again, and there are also poems on the subjects of infertility and menopause. The symptomatic protagonists conjured for the reader might well become patients of one kind or another; and the third section concludes with a series of poems exploring tests, treatments, and surgical procedures.

Poets have written abundantly in recent decades about cancer, dementia, and mental illness, reflecting the predominance and complexity of these varied conditions, and the mixed fortunes of the therapeutic options associated with them. It would have been possible to devote the anthology to poems on these subjects; indeed, as if by a form of indomitability, all three are referenced in multiple sections. The poems in section four converge with the fields of oncology, gerontology, and psychiatry. Also included are poems about brains, headaches, and head injuries, which extend both the portraits of unsettled minds and the beguilingly down-to-earth mode of language that characterises the section as a whole.

There is affinity among the poems in the final section that relates to their ways of approaching illness and healing from standpoints that are less medically and less scientifically inclined than many of the other poems in *Vital Signs*. An octopus heals itself; a horse negotiates its grief at the impending loss of a human companion; a shaman appears in a Galway cardiac drama; apples are cooked to ward off homesickness; a ghostly voice on a remote hill prescribes a cold water remedy; music is identified as being equal to medicine; and poetry itself is understood as a healing vocation, a call to adopt a power of vision that recognises in our suffering, and in our capacity for caring responses, an essence of dignity and a life's purpose.

– **Martin Dyar**

Straight and swift to my wounded I go

PATRICK KAVANAGH

The Hospital

A year ago I fell in love with the functional ward
Of a chest hospital: square cubicles in a row
Plain concrete, wash basins – an art lover's woe,
Not counting how the fellow in the next bed snored.
But nothing whatever is by love debarred,
The common and banal her heat can know.
The corridor led to a stairway and below
Was the inexhaustible adventure of a gravelled yard.

This is what love does to things: the Rialto Bridge,
The main gate that was bent by a heavy lorry,
The seat at the back of a shed that was a suntrap.
Naming these things is the love-act and its pledge;
For we must record love's mystery without claptrap,
Snatch out of time the passionate transitory.

LORNA SHAUGHNESSY

The Dual Citizen

*Everyone who is born holds dual citizenship, in the
kingdom of the well and in the kingdom of the sick.*

— Susan Sontag

Warm assault of forgotten smells.
An antiseptic tingle in the nose,
the vaguely chemical residue of bleach
ignites memory faster than speech –
who you were
before you walked through these doors
who you became and
who you ceased to be
in that year of onerous citizenship.

You find you feel at home
knowing enough of the lingo
to get by and not look a fool,
knowing how to play that part –
how to be the good patient,
take your medicine,
observe routine.

For the next thirty-six hours
you step back into that other self,
become again one among the sick,
recall how it feels to be lucky
 or blessed.

3

PAUL MULDOON

The Field Hospital

Taking, giving back their lives
By the strength of our bare hands,
By the silence of our knives,
We answer to no grey South

Nor blue North. Not self defence,
The lie of just wars, neither
Cold nor hot blood's difference
In their discharging of guns,

But that hillside of fresh graves.
Would this girl brought to our tents
From whose flesh we have removed
Shot that George, on his day off,

Will use to weight fishing lines,
Who died screaming for ether,
Yet protest our innocence?
George lit the lanterns, in danced

Those gigantic, yellow moths
That brushed right over her wounds,
Pinning themselves to our sleeves
Like medals given the brave.

WALT WHITMAN

from The Wound-Dresser

Bearing the bandages, water and sponge,
Straight and swift to my wounded I go,
Where they lie on the ground after the battle brought in,
Where their priceless blood reddens the grass, the ground,
Or to the rows of the hospital tent, or under the roof'd hospital,
To the long rows of cots up and down each side I return,
To each and all one after another I draw near, not one do I miss,
An attendant follows holding a tray, he carries a refuse pail,
Soon to be fill'd with clotted rags and blood, emptied, and fill'd
     again.

I onward go, I stop,
With hinged knees and steady hand to dress wounds,
I am firm with each, the pangs are sharp yet unavoidable,
One turns to me his appealing eyes – poor boy! I never knew you,
Yet I think I could not refuse this moment to die for you, if that
     would save you.

The Nurse

The nurse comes out and tells the boy, *I'm sorry.*
It seems to take all her energy to lift
her slender arm, to place her open palm
gently on the youngster's shoulder, as if to steady

both of them. Perhaps this is her first time
to cross this gap, no watch or jewellery,
her hair tied back, her eyes salt-stung as if
she swam to stand here trembling in the light.

DANNIE ABSE

X-Ray

Some prowl sea-beds, some hurtle to a star
and, mother, some obsessed turn over every stone
or open graves to let that starlight in.
There are men who would open anything.

Harvey, the circulation of the blood,
and Freud, the circulation of our dreams,
pried honourably and honoured are
like all explorers. Men who'd open men.

And those others, mother, with diseases
like great streets named after them: Addison,
Parkinson, Hodgkin – physicians who'd arrive
fast and first at any sour death-bed scene.

I am their slowcoach colleague, half afraid,
incurious. As a boy it was so: you know how
my small hand never teased to pieces
an alarm clock or flensed a perished mouse.

And this larger hand's the same. It stretches now
out from a white sleeve to hold up, mother,
your X-ray to the glowing screen. My eyes look
but don't want to; I still don't want to know.

EMILY DICKINSON

'Surgeons Must Be Very Careful'

Surgeons must be very careful
When they take the knife!
Underneath their fine incisions
Stirs the Culprit – *Life!*

TOM DUDDY

The Touch

If a child fell from a tree, or raved
with fever, or a father came in hurt
from the fields, I was the one who raced
down the roads to the far side of the town,
to the house by the river, glad
of the chance to pass one more time
through the high clanking gates
into the avenue that would slow me

to a crunching walk under the dark,
cher-cherking, rook-swaying canopy.
It never took more than the one
rat-a-tat-tat to bring to the door
the doctor's wife whose briskly gentle hands
once fixed my collar as I stood in the rain.

Sirens

It can't be an accident,
these ambulances
in green and yellow livery
parked on piers and esplanades
while paramedics scan the sea.
What brings them here?

I half expect to see our heroes
strapped to radio masts,
their eardrums stopped with wax,
while bird-bodied nymphs
with difficult names
nest on the rocks hawking cures.

Perhaps Parthenope sings of soothing salt
or Thelxiepeia chants her lists
of seaweeds prized as bandages –
sea oak, sugar kelp, dabberlocks, dulse –
as nurses in wartime
sang the praises of mosses.

Maybe Peisinoe, persuasive as ever,
intones the benefits of seal-bone splints
while Aglaophone ad-libs calypsos
rich with clinical uses
for mermaids' purses.
But this gets complex.

Could it simply be
they feel at home
with ebb and flow,
with peaks and troughs,
with pulsing green,
with crash?

ELIZABETH JENNINGS

Night Sister

How is it possible not to grow hard,
To build a shell around yourself when you
Have to watch so much pain, and hear it too?
Many you see are puzzled, wounded; few
Are cheerful long. How can you not be scarred?

To view a birth or death seems natural,
But these locked doors, these sudden shouts and tears
Graze all the peaceful skies. A world of fears
Like the ghost-haunting of the owl appears.
And yet you love that stillness and that call.

You have a memory for everyone;
None is anonymous and so you cure
What few with such compassion could endure.
I never met a calling quite so pure.
My fears are silenced by the things you've done.

We have grown cynical and often miss
The perfect thing. Embarrassment also
Convinces us we cannot dare to show
Our sickness. But you listen and we know
That you can meet us in our own distress.

MATTHEW SWEENEY

The Doctor's Son

"Look how the doctor's son
sits at the front of the church,
wears a tie every day.
Watch how he smiles
and greets the passers-by
in the mildest way.
Couldn't you think of *him*
instead of the rest of them
when you want to play?
Couldn't you learn
to be a bit like him,
and mind what you say?
I've heard he really swots
while you and your tramp-friends
waste the day.
He'll be a doctor too,
a surgeon perhaps,
while you and them stay
forever round here,
jobless, no doubt,
grown men at play.
Catch hold of yourself,
look at the doctor's boy
and lean that way."

"I see the doctor's son
and I'd very much like
to chuck him into the sea."

CHRISTY BROWN

Old Lady

Miss Mahaffey was her name
all faded lace and silver hair
her face already a skull upon the pillow
lit eerily at night from the streetlight
beaming at the mouth of the narrow lane
below the dull distempered walls of her ward

a frail rainbow fall of silk
faintly smudged at the edges
was little Miss Mahaffey
shrunken and sunken into yesterday
fragile shadow on parched landscape
fingers stirring like limp mice
twitching on the winding shrouds of sheets
maiden lady clinging to grace and dignity
gently lying in her perpetual twilight
not bothering the hurrying nurses for a drop of water
brought by life's meaner barbarities to this
wrinkled and shrivelled up in a crisp bed
coughing up phlegm and speckled blood
being incontinent in the night

a genteel ghost whispering words of no complaint
patient as the plot of earth marked out
to receive her few fish-thin bones

all beauty safely behind her
save briefly when she opened her eyes
to the night nurse bending over her
and murmured "sorry".

MARTINA EVANS

Flowers in the Attic

I hate Dublin and the radiography lectures
and the X-ray department even more,
they laugh at my Cork accent and one
of them said *Aids is a North Side disease.*
I don't want to be here with the snobby girls
with the Donnybrook accents or the registrar
who has nicknamed me *Cork* even though
he is kind. The girl who loves sailing
asks every single one of us what
our fathers do – owning a pub
sounds like something dirty now.
Alone for a moment, I crawl into the shower
with *Flowers in the Attic* and a cinema-sized
bag of Maltesers. Minutes later, Sister
Patricia taps on the door. She smiles
at her fellow Corkonian. I know she cycles
the underground corridors of St Vincent's
in the dark evenings, her white veil flying.
I know she knows a fellow oddball.
Now, Tina.
I hid my trashy book behind my back.
*When you've wiped your face, you'll
have to come back to Nuclear Physics.
The Siemens engineer's been in there
for the last five minutes.* I'm nearly twenty-one,
scared I'm pregnant,
no qualifications, no hope yet,
mournfully following her white habit.

JAMES DICKEY

The Hospital Window

I have just come down from my father.
Higher and higher he lies
Above me in a blue light
Shed by a tinted window.
I drop through six white floors
And then step out onto pavement.

Still feeling my father ascend,
I start to cross the firm street,
My shoulder blades shining with all
The glass the huge building can raise.
Now I must turn round and face it,
And know his one pane from the others.

Each window possesses the sun
As though it burned there on a wick.
I wave, like a man catching fire.
All the deep-dyed windowpanes flash,
And, behind them, all the white rooms
They turn to the colour of Heaven.

Ceremoniously, gravely, and weakly,
Dozens of pale hands are waving
Back, from inside their flames.
Yet one pure pane among these

Is the bright, erased blankness of nothing.
I know that my father is there,

In the shape of his death still living.
The traffic increases around me
Like a madness called down on my head.
The horns blast at me like shotguns,
And drivers lean out, driven crazy –
But now my propped-up father

Lifts his arm out of stillness at last.
The light from the window strikes me
And I turn as blue as a soul,
As the moment when I was born.
I am not afraid for my father –
Look! He is grinning; he is not

Afraid for my life, either,
As the wild engines stand at my knees
Shredding their gears and roaring,
And I hold each car in its place
For miles, inciting its horn
To blow down the walls of the world

That the dying may float without fear
In the bold blue gaze of my father.
Slowly I move to the sidewalk
With my pin-tingling hand half dead
At the end of my bloodless arm.
I carry it off in amazement,

High, still higher, still waving,
My recognised face fully mortal,
Yet not; not at all, in the pale,
Drained, otherworldly, stricken,
Created hue of stained glass.
I have just come down from my father.

An Mhurúch san Ospidéal

Dhúisigh sí
agus ní raibh a heireaball éisc ann
níos mó
ach istigh sa leaba léi
bhí an dá rud fada fuar seo.
Ba dhóigh leat gur gaid mhara iad
nó slaimicí feola.

"Mar mhagadh atá siad
ní foláir,
Oíche na Coda Móire.
Tá leath na foirne as a meabhair
le deoch
is an leath eile acu
róthugtha do jokeanna.
Mar sin féin is leor an méid seo,"
is do chaith sí an dá rud
amach as an seomra.

Ach seo í an chuid
ná tuigeann sí –
conas a thit sí féin ina ndiaidh
'cocs-um-bo-head'.
Cén bhaint a bhí
ag an dá rud léi

nó cén bhaint a bhí aici
leosan?

An bhanaltra a thug an nod di
is a chuir í i dtreo an eolais –
"Cos í seo atá ceangailte díot
agus ceann eile acu anseo thíos fút.
Cos, cos eile
a haon, a dó.

Caithfidh tú foghlaim
conas siúl leo."

Ins na míosa fada
a lean
n'fheadar ar thit a croí
de réir mar a thit
trácht na coise uirthi,
a háirsí?

NUALA NÍ DHOMHNAILL

The Mermaid in the Hospital

She awoke
to find her fishtail
clean gone
but in the bed with her
were two long, cold thingammies.
You'd have thought they were tangles of kelp
or collops of ham.

"They're no doubt
taking the piss,
it being New Year's Eve.
Half the staff legless
with drink
and the other half
playing pranks.
Still, this is taking it
a bit far."
And with that she hurled
the two thingammies out of the room.

But here's the thing
she still doesn't get –
why she tumbled out after them
arse-over-tip ...
How she was connected

to those two thingammies
and how they were connected
to her.

It was the sister who gave her the wink
and let her know what was what.
"You have one leg attached to you there
and another one underneath that.
One leg, two legs ...
A-one and a-two ...
Now you have to learn
what they can do."

In the long months
that followed
I wonder if her heart fell
the way her arches fell,
her instep arches.

– translation of 'An Mhurúch san Ospidéal' by
Paul Muldoon

WAYNE MILLER

Leaving the Hospital

The world beyond the window
was no vaster
than the world inside the room,

just more diffuse. Window
like the screen
of an imaging machine –

on the other side:
luminous, shifting cavities.
(*Stop moving*, I said.)

You looked at me
as though I were an aquarium.
But I was a fist

forced up inside my skull
with no room to unclench.
The nurses

tended to my swollen
bags of saline – lightfilled
syrup, already part of my body,

hanging there.
When they untethered me
at last, I suddenly

was simplified. The doorway
at the end of the long hall
opened onto this

beautiful declivity: my body
was tucked back into me.

BREDA WALL RYAN

Brighid's Eve, Intensive Care

That night I sailed the Islets of Langerhans,
my spinnaker bellied by ionic wind,
rats scavenged casks among the strakes
and fought for purchase on the rigging overhead.
The crew craved rations of Jamaica rum,
molasses, treacle, even bee-laced grog.

Starved ravings edged me overboard,
I dived below the phosphorescent seas,
swam salty underwaters raw as blood –
without a sextant, who could tell the way?
Light oscillated from uncharted stars,
the moons were cobalt, wandering overheard.

Brighid hauled me back on board,
pried open my clenched teeth
and placed the lost electron on my tongue
to summon Panacea and Akeso.
They rafted flotsam from the fevered ship
into a *naomhóg* bound with Brighid's band

lashed fast in double Carrick bends,
unfurled a square sail from her healer's cloak,
then hitched her rushy cross to be our mast.
While Panacea pinned me to the deck,

Akeso helmed us through Delirium Straits,
twisted serpents into oars and rowed ashore.

A trickle of pure oxygen at my ear
and psychotropic histories in my head,
I spent the dog watch on the coral sand.

GERALD DAWE

Going Under

In the Mater I stood at the big window
and looked at the courtyard far below.

Nuns at night hovered down long halls
of bed-ridden men who often called.

Beside me, one of them grinned:
What are you in for? Can't be as bad

as this? And proudly showed off
his wall-less eye. *Quit that, you'll terrify*

the boy, another said. Then I was
wheeled off and, under the soft mask,

counted into oblivion. When I woke
the rough linen sheets were flecked with blood.

DERMOT HEALY

Recovery

in memory of Charlie McGovern

I

The first thing I hear is women's voices,
the next a priest withdrawing from me.
A friend leaves by the bedside
Berryman's 'Eleven Addresses to the Lord'
which I must have asked for

and then you
climb in the window

(funny to fall asleep at last
in the women's ward and outside
the drunken gardener falling
asleep under
the purple plum).

II

Night nurses water the flowers;
St Joseph guards my window,
a giant shadow thrown across the room at night in prayer.
And after being moved from the women's ward
they find room for me in the men's.

Charlie, after a lifetime of coughing,
lies across from me.

You can make any tree weep, he explains,
if you train it. A man in the corridor drops dead
after weighing himself on the scales.
Did the second hand register his soul leaving,
flying off? And a woman is saying:
It will be easy to satisfy me now,
I wouldn't dream of spending
half the night up now,
oh God, no.

III

When your head begins to swing to the right
we'll correct the tendency,
when your head begins to swing to the left
just shout for me, the doctor said,

and then the veins begin to gather
like gnarled roots
at the back of my head.

IV

You're one of the lucky ones, says the doctor,
usually they die.
The one sure thing is
it can never happen to you again.
That's something, I suppose,
I say.

V

In a local news item in the *Anglo-Celt*
a man is described who died
after receiving a prick
from a rose in his garden;

the following week
his brother was shot by gangsters
in New York.

So what do you make of news like that?
I feel like Virginia Woolf
when she stood under the vast dome of the British Museum

and felt as if she were a single thought
in that huge broad forehead.

VI

How many thoughts can one cram into a day?
How many of us are in this world
rising up and doing a little,
going some of the way,
being there at the time,
in the early morning meeting them
down the side streets,
the sound of shoes, steps being washed down,
coal being dropped into a hole in the street?

An example of sublime scepticism
is the man who discovered purgatory.

Charlie McGovern,
after a lifetime in the Air Force
where he saw coffins come back from Vietnam
filled with dope,
left his apartment in the States,
just turned the key in the lock,
and came home to die in Ireland.

And then today
Charlie McGovern
saw an X-ray of his lung
which he prayed was not his,
one big white mushroom

rising over Glengevlin.

VII

Poor Charlie,
highest nut in the wood,
man of the limestone-white neck,
now you are heartbroken and fallen on hard times

a herb of grace is needed for your wound
or young women who in the heat-haze of noon
might pluck for you *moonógs*
from down at the black rocks;

not for show you constantly shrug your shoulders
and stay awake most of the night,
your last horse stands in the gorse haggard
looking at the same spot for days,

your dogs have strayed from you
to the Maguires and the O'Rourkes
and sometimes you stop at the gate
watching for them, whistling,

and Pilib, when winter freshened his wound,
departed beyond the wounded Boyne,
he sends neither message nor friends to bring good news,
but the heart has only what it is accustomed to,

so you follow with affection tales of his,
news of great victories,
thousands of foreigners dead,
while in your innermost heart

you found the shaft
enter his heart,
and his memory in your mind
will long be a reproach to you –

Pilib, breathless in death,
propped up in his coffin
like in the prow of a currach.
Afterwards you cross through Dowra

like a man astray in the head
and try luring birds from the cliffs
that you might have some sign of the future,
acknowledgements from the blackfaced queen

that she might send you easy peace terms.
But the news is not good.
The last time I saw you you were trying to sit up in the Home.
They were shooting the hereafter into your veins.

VIII

In the miraculous country of silk
where the horse runs with one foot
poised on the wings of a swallow

and the natives refrain from saying
the names of women who are called by the names of flowers
or the names of men who are called by the names of birds

lest they awake a sleeping ancestor,
so, Charlie, I say your name low.
As I recovered you were dying,

the priest suddenly came out from behind the screen,
and across sand and muffled stones
the undercurrent bore your soul away.

IX

In Killygowen
all rested and well
I feel another
heart beating by my side,
joy all round.

The first day I go to town
an off-duty soldier speaking of grief
congratulated me
with a flick of his fingers.
"I saw you at the funeral,"

he says.
I look at him a long time
trying to gauge who has died.
"It was good of you," he says, "to come."
"It was nothing," I replied.

ROBERT BURNS

To Dr. Maxwell, On Miss Jessy Staig's Recovery

Maxwell, if merit here you crave,
That merit I deny;
You save fair Jessie from the grave! –
An Angel could not die.

AIDEEN HENRY

Waiting Room

The old lady sighs, looks into space,
conflicting signals
in her forehead and eyebrows.
She did not sleep last night.

Her young companion oscillates
between attending to her
and to a bleating mobile phone,
whose texts pierce like the cry of a newborn.

She is a niece;
none of the tensions of a daughter.
Her voice shows gentle fondness,
her face hidden behind the beige mask.

Her young body tightly coiled,
leans forwards to hold the old lady's hand,
and her sacral tattoo sneaks a look out
below her jacket.

They speak of Martha who died;
that she did not fight it, that her acceptance
made her passage easier, that her best friend
had written a poem that would make a stone cry.

WILLIAM CARLOS WILLIAMS

Complaint

They call me and I go.
It is a frozen road
past midnight, a dust
of snow caught
in the rigid wheeltracks.
The door opens.
I smile, enter and
shake off the cold.
Here is a great woman
on her side in the bed.
She is sick,
perhaps vomiting,
perhaps labouring
to give birth to
a tenth child. Joy! Joy!
Night is a room
darkened for lovers,
through the jalousies the sun
has sent one gold needle!
I pick the hair from her eyes
and watch her misery
with compassion.

SEAMUS HEANEY

Out of the Bag

1

All of us came in Doctor Kerlin's bag.
He'd arrive with it, disappear to the room
And by the time he'd reappear to wash

Those nosy, rosy, big, soft hands of his
In the scullery basin, its lined insides
(The colour of a spaniel's inside lug)

Were empty for all to see, the trap-sprung mouth
Unsnibbed and gaping wide. Then like a hypnotist
Unwinding us, he'd wind the instruments

Back into their lining, tie the cloth
Like an apron round itself,
Darken the door and leave

With the bag in his hand, a plump ark by the keel ...
Until the next time came and in he'd come
In his fur-lined collar which was also spaniel-coloured

And go stooping up to the room again, a whiff
Of disinfectant, a Dutch interior gleam
Of waistcoat satin and highlights on the forceps.

Getting the water ready, that was next –
Not plumping hot, and not lukewarm, but soft,
Sud-luscious, saved for him from the rain-butt

And savoured by him afterwards, all thanks
Denied as he towelled hard and fast,
Then held his arms out suddenly behind him

To be squired and silk-lined into the camel coat.
At which point he once turned his eyes upon me,
Hyperborean, beyond-the-north wind blue,

Two peepholes to the locked room I saw into
Every time his name was mentioned, skimmed
Milk and ice, swabbed porcelain, the white

And chill of tiles, steel hooks, chrome surgery tools
And blood dreeps in the sawdust where it thickened
At the foot of each cold wall. And overhead

The little, pendent, teat-hued infant parts
Strung neatly from a line up near the ceiling –
A toe, a foot and shin, an arm, a cock

A bit like the rosebud in his buttonhole.

2

Poeta doctus Peter Levi says
Sanctuaries of Asclepius (called *asclepions*)
Were the equivalent of hospitals

In ancient Greece. Or of shrines like Lourdes,
Says *poeta doctus* Graves. Or of the cure
By poetry that cannot be coerced,

Say I, who realised at Epidaurus
That the whole place was a sanatorium
With theatre and gymnasium and baths,

A site of incubation, where 'incubation'
Was technical and ritual, meaning sleep
When epiphany occurred and you met the god …

Hatless, groggy, shadowing myself
As the thurifer I was in an open-air procession
In Lourdes in '56

When I nearly fainted from the heat and fumes,
Again I nearly fainted as I bent
To pull a bunch of grass and hallucinated

Doctor Kerlin at the steamed-up glass
Of the scullery window, starting in to draw
With his large pink index finger dot-faced men

With button-spots in a straight line down their fronts
And women with dot breasts, giving them all
A set of droopy sausage-arms and legs

That soon began to run. And then as he dipped and laved
In the generous suds again, *miraculum*:
The baby bits all came together swimming

Into his soapy big hygienic hands
And I myself came to, blinded with sweat,
Blinking and shaky in the windless light.

3

Bits of the grass I pulled I posted off
To one going in to chemotherapy
And one who had come through. I didn't want

To leave the place or link up with the others.
It was midday, mid-May, pre-tourist sunlight
In the precincts of the god,

The very site of the temple of Asclepius.
I wanted nothing more than to lie down
Under hogweed, under seeded grass

And to be visited in the very eye of the day
By Hygeia, his daughter, her name still clarifying
The haven of light she was, the undarkening door.

4

The room I came from and the rest of us all came from
Stays pure reality where I stand alone,
Standing the passage of time, and she's asleep

In sheets put on for the doctor, wedding presents
That showed up again and again, bridal
And usual and useful at births and deaths.

Me at the bedside, incubating for real,
Peering, appearing to her as she closes
And opens her eyes, then lapses back

Into a faraway smile whose precinct of vision
I would enter every time, to assist and be asked
In that hoarsened whisper of triumph,

"And what do you think
Of the new wee baby the doctor brought for us all
When I was asleep?"

MAEVE O'SULLIVAN

Haiku

a young girl
smoothes her mother's hair back –
Outpatients

Instead of dying,
they inject you with sunlight and you live

MARY O'DONNELL

Doctors, Daughters

My mother's small face is wreathed
and criss-crossed by fear. She has
no time for food or sleep.

Away from the hospital,
she rails at us her daughters,
who can do nothing,

her days layered with quests for solutions.
This man, whose pyjamas she irons
and re-buttons, which she brings to him

laundered and crisp, to whom she carries
perfect nectarines, cranberry juice,
is failing her. She wards off visitors

lest they witness his decline,
frantic to capture an antidote,
that special inscribed phial,

to bear it back in her hands
from monstrous caves like a magical gift,
past nurses, past mulling consultants

and, having fought, to shout in scorn:
"See? Fools!" Her every word,
attests to the uselessness of doctors

and daughters, who cannot heal.

WILLIAM BUTLER YEATS

A Friend's Illness

Sickness brought me this
Thought, in that scale of his:
Why should I be dismayed
Though flame had burned the whole
World, as it were a coal,
Now I have seen it weighed
Against a soul?

DIANE SEUSS

'I saw a little movie of a person stroking'

I saw a little movie of a person stroking a small bird with two
    Q-tips, one held between
the forefinger and thumb of each hand. It tipped back its head
    to receive the minor
tenderness, which to the bird must have felt like being touched
    by a god. For a moment
I knew what it would be to feel at the mercy of love, small-
    scale, the kind shown but not
spoken of. I was afraid to touch you. I was afraid of the lesions
    you'd described to me
over the phone, their locations and the measurement, in
    centimetres, of each. Jesus-marks
you called them. All so I would be prepared and unafraid or
    less afraid but still I was afraid
of dying like you were dying. When I first arrived I looked so
    long into your eyes you
shivered and ordered me to look away. You were imperious in
    your dying yet courtly
about my fear, you understood, as if I were a child afraid of
    lightning storms, which I am,
having at age ten been struck. Out of the blue you said that
    once you were dead I'd never
be able to listen to *Blue* again, Joni Mitchell's *Blue*, not just the
    song but the whole album.
It was a minor curse you lay across my shoulders like a fur
    dyed blue, and so I listen now
in defiance of you. In the listening the pronouns shift. We are
    listening. There is no death.

MICHAEL HARTNETT

That Actor Kiss

I kissed my father as he lay in bed
in the ward. Nurses walked on soles of sleep
and old men argued with themselves all day.
The seven decades locked inside his head
congealed into a timeless leaking heap,
the painter lost his sense of all but grey.
That actor kiss fell down a shaft too deep
to send back echoes that I would have prized –
'29 was '41 was '84,
all one in his kaleidoscopic eyes
(he willed to me his bitterness and thirst,
his cold ability to close a door).
Later, over a drink, I realised
that was our last kiss and, alas, our first.

died 3 October 1984

VICTORIA KENNEFICK

Diet

In the hospital, my father ate tubs of high-calorie
strawberry-flavoured meal-replacement.
Occasionally, vanilla. Sometimes, they brought
meals under plastic covers with stewed tea.
The whole ward a nightmare of hard-boiled eggs
and jelly. He would have starved
were we not on-call to lift up his head in our hands,
talk nonsense, distract him from the truth
of how he was living. With his eyes shut, he opened
his mouth a little, so we fed him with tiny spoons.
How could he eat it, this gloopy mass, sliming
the carton? In truth, I fell out of love with food
because my father did. It was summer, I remember.
I wanted to pick life from trees, wellness from bushes,
huge bunches of health from the garden and hold them
to his lips so he could taste sun, air, light, his life
still throbbing in my veins. But everything died
when I brought it inside that room. Still
I marvel how death turned me too to bone.

LEANNE O'SULLIVAN

Lightning

No wind, no rain, but every bolt that staggered
from the cumulus that night seemed to raise
a frenzy in the hemispheres of his brain.

I held my husband's head in the damp nest
of my palms, watched the tremors in his eyes
turn and turn like tiny whirlwinds, until

all that I loved was lost in lightning, darkness,
fire. And when the anaesthetic began
to ferry him down a calmer circle,

to wait out the night, I praised his strength,
the goodness of his body – every working cell
and keeper of his passage I prayed defend him,

I let him go. Near midnight the nurse shone
her torch over the still lakes of his eyes,
and I thought of sleeping Odysseus safe beneath

his quilt of leaves, his face smooth like wax-paper,
no piercing rain, no drenched gales or beating heat
upon him. No movement, she said. No light.

LELAND BARDWELL

A Mother Mourns Her Heroin-Addicted Daughter

How could I have dreamt
That my bird of paradise,
My green-clad hippie girl,
Could be so reduced
To the gammon face of poverty,
The incessant whinge of a child.

If we rolled up time like a ball
I'd give you the cherries of my nipples,
I'd wash you almond clean
And lay your hair like lint
On the cartilage of my breast.

A prey to the barren street, you're lost
On the breach of years that no silk
Nor cotton drawing-to of threads
Can mend. The void. Your path is marked
Like gull-prints on an empty beach.

The drug has perished your will.
You float like a stick on a pond
In here, in there – to a harbour of lily-trees,
Or held for days in scum till the light
Breeze lifts you and you edge along.

Will you walk on my street once more?
I'll raise my pavements to keep you safe,
Open the balcony of my arms.
I will buckle your shoes again
And shine the mirror for your dance.

But you will not throw away your bag of tricks.
Your monkey fingers cling to the safety net
In which you nightly land, having walked
The trembling wire and heard the screams
Of anticipation, seen the up-turned mouths.

How can we melt down the glaciers
Of days, the furnaces of night?

SENI SENEVIRATNE

For My Father

It was a little like –
black water, like lonely, like hungry,

his boyhood. No wonder
he needed something stronger,

something, not bone-like
(though bones are strong), something

before calcium, something
to pull him away, something

other-worldly – a watchful eye
in the clouds, a hand pulling him towards

the old woman she would have been,
were it not for, were it not for –.

Let's say he was a boy and
he walked without a mother.

Like medicine, the years
between. Long enough to dull

the first cut. Door on door
opened and closed but she was

always somewhere else,
as if winnowed to oblivion.

JULIE O'CALLAGHAN

from Sketches for an Elegy

Jack and I are resting
under a weeping willow
beside the beach
I want to stop
asking silly questions
and talk about
important topics
such as
which colour he likes best

***

it could ruin
a person's outlook
on a jaunty
August morning
to wake up and hear
the Death March on WFMT
and then see
your ghostly bald father
facing the music
at the table
attempting to eat
a bowl of Cheerios

***

staring from his bed,
he asked, "How long
did that doctor say?
Was it nine to ten months?
Or was it eight to twelve?"
when I told him six to eight
he shook his head
"Just look at that sky"

***

a cold start to the summer –
everything was haywire
mist all over the skyscrapers
and no customers
down at the beach

***

we stood in the park
looking for exotic migrating birds
resting on their way north
for the summer
yellow and blue and red birds
everywhere

***

sitting around
the chemotherapy room
for hours
I read all the magazines – twice
listening to the others
talk about the price of wigs
the great plumber
they had found

★★★

Sunday in August
nothing much doing
we go and get groceries
you need a bench to rest on
so we head for the beach
between the skyscrapers
once you feel better
we take off our shoes
and wade in the lake

★★★

a lunatic in the bank
telling the cashier
her life story
– poor bugger
you say

***

you pull me over and whisper
"See this guy. I've known him for years
– watch what happens when we pass by"
nothing
"Nobody recognises me anymore"

ELAINE FEENEY

Egg

When the fourth doctor said

your son is an egg cracked by a hammer

I thought how no-one makes an
omelette

    without cracking

you heard the vicious
onomatopoeic word
as a terrible screaming

so now darlings

let us break everything up

(like she did to a life's work)

I offer you this

crack is needed to be born

ed is somewhat unfixable

therefore let us settle on the
hammer's potential
to build

PAULA CUNNINGHAM

A History of Snow

It was wild sudden.
Her daddy phoned me to work.
She was that hot he just had a sheet over her.
I felt the heat before I lifted the sheet and seen the rash.

You'd never forget that rash.
People say to me "How would you know?"
and I just say "You'd know if you seen it."
Purple.

The wee spots and these big blotches like birthmarks –
everywhere only her face.
Her wee lady and all.
I phoned and they said do the glass test.

I pressed really hard
and her bawling, but it didn't change
so we brung her up.
There was this old man in the queue

very wheezy, he said to the girl
"I want them to see this child
before they see me."
And within two minutes we're in the ambulance.

She was bouncing up and down on the trolley,
you wouldn't believe it. Like something
out of *The Exorcist*. The doctor come
and he told us prepare for the worst.

She's a bit of hearing loss, that's all,
in big rooms, like, but she's grand.
They say it'll all come right, the ear adjusts.
Her daddy brung her in snow in a lunchbox –

she'd never seen it before.
They'd pushed her cot right up to the window,
the flakes sweeping past like confetti,
a bit of a rose in her cheeks, and her all eyes.

The cars in the car park were buried in minutes,
it was one snowy evening, the whole
of the country froze. She'd been in four weeks
and I mind she was eating an orange –

a mandarin one of the nurses had peeled.
That's when I knew she really was on the mend.
They said if we'd even been five minutes later.
I think of that old man yet.

AOIFE LYALL

Treasure Island

Unadorned but for the clip
on your umbilical cord, we are
skin to skin.

The blue paper curtain
oceans our island. It is full of treasure.

Here is my mother's necklace, unclasped
and heirloomed in cotton wool.

Here, the watch my father gave me:
how easily time slides and twists
over a naked wrist.

Here, my wedding-rings take the light
and with it their pledge and promise.
I lay them aside and lift you

to my chest, my treasure. There,
you unlock my motherself
and find it full of riches.

JESSICA TRAYNOR

Anatomy Scan

Let's begin with a shroud, darkened by time,
pushed aside to show your bones' filigree.
The ultrasound probes and digs as you slither
in and out of focus, sockets gaping
like a Halloween ghost through a sheet.
The hole of your stomach. The chomp
of your heartbeat hungering below my gut.
Perfect cerebellum. A very nice spine.
There – the kidneys. Little dark pockets of need.
Colour flares across the screen, arterial flow
through widening chambers, its rush exhausting.
The eyeball's orbit. Closed but watchful.
Your twig arms flinch and flick. Your tiny jaws grin.
Little lizard. You know something I've forgotten.

HARRY CLIFTON

A Son! A Son!

You around whom, at every hour,
The void thickens like an atmosphere
Rank with unsolved mystery, childish fears,

Go back now, through the Dublin lanes
To that very first year
Of malt and drayhorse, Francis Street, the Coombe.

Two women wait, in an ante-room.
A man who has crashed the lights
At Cuffe Street in the small hours, in the rain,

Chainsmokes endlessly – Players cigarettes.
Doctor Kidney, hedging his bets
And slapping nurses' bottoms, flashes through

In a white housecoat, the local deity.
Yes, we must all be patient,
Even you, in the ageless womb,

In the shadow of Saint Nicholas of Myra,
Where salt waits, oil in its cruse.
You will find your own way out of this maze

Of headscarves, factory whistles, cheap red meat
And dark soutanes on Thomas Street –
The fifties ... Then as now,

To be hung upside down, on a brilliant scales,
A thumbprint on your brow,
Is all you know. And the old wives' tales

In the ante-room, the man dissolving in tears
Who has just become your father,
Lost in a fog of years.

DOIREANN NÍ GHRÍOFA

Inventory: Recovery Room

A thin yellow curtain shivers around my bed.
The IV stand bows its metal head
and a clipboard displays falling numbers.

On the windowsill, empty-eyed bottles stare at rain.
A plastic plug lies on the tile, severing TV from socket.
The screen is black now and shows only my reflection:

pale face, blue gown, surgical socks stretched up to the crotch.
My breasts are funnelled into plastic cups. The machine
whine-whirrs, stretches my flesh, lets go again;

the feeling as strange as a pinned and needled leg.
Still, nothing happens
until I think of milk, of beestings squeezed from a cow's udders,

of my fingers between a calf's gums: the fierce suck of a new mouth,
and the echo of a mother's angry bellows from the field.
Within my chest, an itch begins to stir. The machine's slow suck

and release yields a single drop of yellow liquid.
A second slow drop forms and falls ... Another.
Another. I sit and feed the machine, politely, quietly.

Electricity pulls milk from me as I continue my inventory –
by the wall, an empty cot, a hand-knit blanket,
a small white hat and an unused nappy, flat.

RÓISÍN TIERNEY

Ataxia

Your first wobbles they put down to wobbliness
in general. Then your many falls and tumbles
raised the red flag for danger,
sent them hurtling for a diagnosis,
which took its time coming: ataxia
– O elegant word! – from the Greek,
meaning lack of order (in your case, balance),
progressive, degenerative, part of you.

Your unsteady sway naturally caused problems
when it came to casting for the school play
(*The Owl and the Pussycat*, we were still primary),
until Mrs Galassy or Mrs Cox –
whose kindly stroke of genius was it? –
placed you upheld between two other girls,
each holding an arm, firmly,
all swaying in unison, as the West Wind,
and intoning the chorus
(something like "Blow wind, whoo HOO!"),
while we in the audience, your parents and sisters,
laughed at your shenanigans up on the stage,
rolled around in our laughter like a windswept sea.

CIAN FERRITER

Limbo

The ward reduces to its midnight hush.
A week since you were born six weeks too soon,

we keep vigil in this touch-less limbo.
Your face a miniature in distance,

your fingers gripping invisible lines.
Deirdre expressing to your silent cries.

In the small hours, without a word, a nurse
releases you into your mother's arms.

Sensing your breath in that titanic hold,
I wrap my shaking self around you both.

LAUREN HALDEMAN

from Instead of Dying

Instead of dying, you move in with us. We fix the basement up with a shower & a small area for your bed & you come to live. I help you carry boxes down the stairs. We set up your record player. We hang up your old poster from 5th grade that says 'Save the Wolves'. Once a week, you make grilled cheese for us in the upstairs kitchen. Instead of dying, instead of being stabbed on the street in Denver, instead of bleeding to death surrounded by strangers neither you nor I will ever meet, instead of all that, you get a job at the local grocery store, stocking the shelves, watering the produce: collards, endive, grapefruit. Your face stays your face & your pain gets better & you swim at the Rec Centre in the early light of spring & you are so not not not dead.

Instead of dying, they inject you with sunlight & you live. It is a highly experimental process developed in the deep caverns of Luray, where a fluid from the crevices of the previous earth is found to contain a slow conglomerate of sunlight. Scientists discover they can separate the plasma into a medicinal dose, a shot of which can bring a boy back from death after being stabbed three times in the chest. *The Belt of Orion*, they call it. And it works. The moment the needle goes into your arm, you open your eyes. The bright light enters your bloodstream. And we thank the doctors and the ambulance drivers and even the man who did this to you, since he provided us with the opportunity to infuse you with infinite illumination.

EILÉAN NÍ CHUILLEANÁIN

The Polio Epidemic

No hurry at all in house or garden,
The children were kept from the danger –
The parents suddenly had more time
To watch them, to keep them amused,
To see they had plenty to read.
The city lay empty, infected.
There was no more ice-cream.
The baths were closed all summer.

One day my father allowed me beyond the gate
With a message to pass through a slit in a blank wall;
I promised I would just cycle for two hours,
Not stop or talk, and I roamed the long roads
Clear through city and suburbs, past new churches,
Past ridges of houses where strange children
Were kept indoors too, I sliced through miles of air,
Free as a plague angel descending
On places the buses went: Commons Road, Friars' Walk.

ENDA WYLEY

Through the Window

for my mother

Odd but necessary the solution that comes to us,
to stare through glass at you: your parched face
slanted towards the afternoon light. On your wall
a forest you'd painted when we were young.

Two red coated figures walk under trees
and we remember the bedtime story you read us –
wardrobe portal into snow, a lamppost, Narnia's wood.
Now, here is the masked carer, opening the window

to the love we yell in – such force it unsettles you.
We're ready to turn back to our strange world
where we stand apart, can't touch, but lucky
we've seen your lips pucker into one last kiss.

Athoscailt

Is é an cleas atá ann an righneas mínádúrtha,
an seasamh siar a chur díot láithreach, gan aon riail á sárú.
Má tá tú istigh leo, ní chuirfear cnámh ann.

Caithfidh an fear atá scoite ón mbeár mála Tayto leat
le tabhairt dá shípéir Gearmánach – Dante –
is nuair a fhiafróidh a chompánach de

ar osclaíodh prochóg éigin faoin mbaile mór, an bhfuil
oisrí anois á riar acu,
is ar mhaithe leatsa chomh maith le héinne
a labhróidh an guth taobh thiar den chuntar, *Tá sin... oisrí*
agus super noodles.

AIFRIC MAC AODHA

Reopening

The trick will be to slip off the bridle
as soon as you can without breaking the rules. If
you catch it, you'll know in your marrow.

The man ringfenced from the bar will toss you a bag
of Tayto to give to his German Shepherd – Dante –
and when his other pal asks if some dive

in town is open, and if they're serving oysters now,
for your benefit as much as anyone else's
the voice from behind the counter will say, *They are ...*
oysters and super noodles.

– translation of 'Athoscailt' by **David Wheatley**

NICK NORWOOD

Mumps

Four weeks farmed out to the farm
when I was four years old,
my sister down with mumps, my parents jobs:
"You'll be better off with your grandparents."

Quickly, we three fell to: checking
below thumbed earlobes
for signs of swelling, a bucket by my antique
iron-frame bed, pointed questions.

Meanwhile, my grandfather got a crop
of cotton in and trailered it to gin,
my grandmother clerked in the town grocery.
I paced among the aisles,

stood in awe of the butcher's blood,
his cleaver and apron. The dark barn drew me
to the old man's side, a finger through
the hammer loop

of his pinstripe overalls. The cows
followed us in the pickup,
necks stretched, bawling. By eight
the whole world was black

and still as the yard itself. The house
ticked. I'd hear a rat scrabble,

a pair of owls sounding the distance
between one burr oak and another,

and breathe, in 1966, the modest,
stored-up air of the 1930s, taste,
by day, the tinniness of a cistern,
earthenness of a garden.

Until the coast seemed clear, I hadn't
got it, and they started
packing me to leave one still-dark
morning in a rain so hard

my grandfather laid a gangplank across
the flooded yard to reach the car,
then came back to find me in the kitchen,
suddenly swollen,

the contents of my stomach rolling
across the floor's warped, tilting
linoleum – the flotsam
of a desperate, storm-wracked sea –

as if the mumps had found the cure
for me, and not the other way
around, and granted me four more
weeks on that healing ground.

NUALA NÍ CHONCHÚIR

Scamhóga Áille

Ritheann siad tharam,
dúshúileach,
fadsciortach,
le craiceann chomh mín
le dealbh den Mhaighdean.
Tá siad ag sú ar thoitíní
cosúil le leanbh ar líreacán,
is ritheann sé liom:
'Bhur scamhóga,
bhur scamhóga,
bhur scamhóga áille'.
Ach tuigim go dtógfaidh sé
deich mbliana nó níos mó orthu
aon mhachnamh a dhéanamh.

NUALA NÍ CHONCHÚIR

Pink Lungs

When they clatter past,
all gothic-eyed
and hippy-dressed,
with skin as pure
as a plaster Virgin,
you watch them cup fag ends,
suck on them like inhalers,
and all you can think is
'Your lungs, your lungs,
your pretty pink lungs',
and you know it'll
take them a decade,
or longer, to even begin
to think about it.

– translation of 'Scamhóga Áille' by the author

PAUL McCARRICK

Stop and Love the People

There is enough unbalance in the world.
Stars remain aligned, but compasses twirl.
You think in stammers of the past, the present,
and the magpies impinging your future.
You think just enough to keep wheels spinning,
arms moving, cars driven, evenings bearable.
There are ways to distract from the thinking.
Horticulture, journaling, cookery, and the versatile
self-abuse of drinking. And walking –
the alpha and omega of any given day,
the movement in lines within intimate, metrical circles.
When all sunsets over the Shannon or south Roscommon
have blended into one, you will learn that you just have to stop
and love the people, because there is nothing else to be done.

KAREN J. McDONNELL

My Grandfather Battles Death

Stanislaus
Perhaps I remembered the story
of the boy-uncle who slipped
on the way home
from Count McCormack's concert
and of the Tipperary woman who
wiped the mud off his suit.

Young enough to ask
the unaskable, I did: "Grandad,
how did he die?"
and watched my grandfather
disappear in front of me.

Slipping out in space to
where his oldest son fought
delirium and the bedclothes
on his eighth birthday,
and the good doctor was saying
"Meningitis".

"He gave a scream, and he died,"
Grandad said, to no one, though
he had answered my question
and I was still at his side.

In those minutes, a witness.
His confidant.

The Hidden Child
Scarlatina was rampant.
In the fever hospital, Limerick's
quarantined children waved
to parents from upstairs windows.

My grandfather would not give up
his second son. The good doctor said
"Keep him isolated, and I'll let him
stay at home."
The boy told the fireside story
seventy years later,

and I saw him then, my grandfather:
a rare knight in a gas mask,
his spiky white hair gilded
by the sulphur bomb purge
of the invalid's room. Emerging
from Death's smoky arena –
Victorious.

The Cancer Ward
School-holiday July. In the cancer ward
Death sat on my grandfather's chest,
leering at nurses and teenage girls,
inviting proximity, blowing hot
on tear ducts.

Pausing on the carbolic-scented
battlefield, Grandad took a deep
breath, then exhaled
"Are you alright for money?"

My father set me free
with a nod of the head but
tears came at the door and
Death's crowing laughter barrelled
along the waxed corridor rubbing
past me on the terrazzo stairs.

KEITH JARRETT

Parasites

When I was twenty-one or maybe it was
twenty-two amoebas multiplied the pain of it

I left for home lighter much lighter though tropical
sun turned my shade to black my own mother didn't

last year at the hospital lab parasites rediscovered
in my stools sit with this a little while so much time

hidden settling unsettling one is transitive one in-transit
I am saying only what those microscopes saw not what I

felt so much so many years of unsettling so gut me in my
feeling so many poisoned rivers so sad when they said unto

me I had been carrying these Caribbean waters all these years
gut refugees fed an old world diet I will not say contaminated

I would rather carry a billion billion times more for I am hosting
their stories and I have never felt this empty this bitter this so help me.

DEREK MAHON

Everything Is Going
to Be All Right

How should I not be glad to contemplate
the clouds clearing beyond the dormer window
and a high tide reflected on the ceiling?
There will be dying, there will be dying,
but there is no need to go into that.
The lines flow from the hand unbidden
and the hidden source is the watchful heart;
the sun rises in spite of everything
and the far cities are beautiful and bright.
I lie here in a riot of sunlight
watching the day break and the clouds flying.
Everything is going to be all right.

We're here in the terrain of sheets

MAYA C. POPA

The Bees Have Been Cancelled

Never again the humming, saddled flowers. Never the
blind oath by a velveteen prisoner. Never the yellow, hula
hooped in black, little engine left running late into the
darkness. Oh, how they were charming, clever monographs.
Sunlight couldn't save them from the angel of extinction.
Virgil said they swell with nectar's tilted knowledge. I don't
know what to believe. Maybe they tired of being addicts.
Clover honey, garbage honey, accidental ice cream honey.
Ransomed stamen, sweetsinful will-do-anything-for honey.
Maybe they caught fevers at midnight with no one there to
hold their stingers, no fat queen to press a cold compress.
How will we currency honey from wildflowers, that liquid of
languages? How pollinate in the bees' electrostatic absence?
How will the bellbirds take it, the Canterbury birds?
Who will cast the last skeleton in amber? I'll miss the noise,
the palimpsestic clamour, soft shock of discovering a hive
under your roof. The lull as each integer walked its body
over a blossom, then flew away with its instructions.

Mental Cases

Who are these? Why sit they here in twilight?
Wherefore rock they, purgatorial shadows,
Drooping tongues from jaws that slob their relish,
Baring teeth that leer like skulls' tongues wicked?
Stroke on stroke of pain, – but what slow panic,
Gouged these chasms round their fretted sockets?
Ever from their hair and through their hand palms
Misery swelters. Surely we have perished
Sleeping, and walk hell; but who these hellish?

– These are men whose minds the Dead have ravished.
Memory fingers in their hair of murders,
Multitudinous murders they once witnessed.
Wading sloughs of flesh these helpless wander,
Treading blood from lungs that had loved laughter.
Always they must see these things and hear them,
Batter of guns and shatter of flying muscles,
Carnage incomparable and human squander
Rucked too thick for these men's extrication.

Therefore still their eyeballs shrink tormented
Back into their brains, because on their sense
Sunlight seems a bloodsmear; night comes blood-black;
Dawn breaks open like a wound that bleeds afresh.
– Thus their heads wear this hilarious, hideous,

Awful falseness of set-smiling corpses.
– Thus their hands are plucking at each other;
Picking at the rope-knouts of their scourging;
Snatching after us who smote them, brother,
Pawing us who dealt them war and madness.

MIROSLAV HOLUB

Casualty

They bring us crushed fingers,
mend it, doctor.
They bring burnt-out eyes,
hounded owls of hearts,
they bring a hundred white bodies,
a hundred red bodies,
a hundred black bodies,
mend it, doctor,
on the dishes of ambulances they bring
the madness of blood
the scream of flesh,
the silence of charring,
mend it, doctor.

And while we are suturing
inch after inch,
night after night,
nerve to nerve,
muscle to muscle,
eyes to sight,
they bring in
even longer daggers,
even more thunderous bombs,
even more glorious victories,

idiots.

KERRIE O'BRIEN

Cleanse

I heard a man talk of it once –
At the end of every mission
They order them into the sea
Where nothing is forgotten
In salt light
Stripped bare
Going in slowly –
Shy, almost
After the filth of war
The heat
All of it caught
In their eyes
They stand
Facing the light
As if for the first time

HANNAH COPLEY

An Archive

Named Extreme Cure, or, On the Misnomer
of the term Heroic Medicine. There is a rolling stack

dedicated to the wax each child dons to face the crowned light.
Cabinets for all the coaxed substances: colostrum, milk, placenta,

the shed lining of a womb. A microfilm that discusses how blood
can cover a table and a floor without the presence of a blade.

One file records how pushing is its own emetic – during,
and later, gingerly, amidst a fractured tailbone and each raw wound.

There is a city of death certificates, with new tower blocks
built every year, and a room with an ancient projector that loops a film

on how the women used to midwife and do still. Thirty hours
of work produces forty-eight centimetres of bawling result;

of vellum skin tucked into its proper place. See in this file
this spooling marvel of vernix and flesh.

NANDI JOLA

Brussels (Will Fix Me)

She pierced through my virginity
blade on one hand
other stroking my cornrowed hair
I wet myself
blood gushing down my tender thighs
he looks at me as a husband does
I look at him intimately
I feel nothing
he speaks
not even the scent of rose water
or pomegranate perfume I bathed in
I can't make him stay
Brussels is where they stitch girls like me
fix me.

CELIA DE FRÉINE

Cailís mo Chuid Fola

Dá mbeadh a fhios agam
agus sinn ag súgradh sa chlós

nárbh ionann m'fhuilse
is fuil na ngirseach eile

go raibh mo chorpsa
fós á chothú ag fuil iasachta

d'fhéadfainn guí
go sciobfaí uaim an chailís seo

d'fhéadfainn a ghealladh dom féin
sula dtitfinn i ngrá

go meallfainn mo rogha fir
trí ghréasán an ospidéil

chun a fháil amach ar fheil muid dá chéile
is nuair nár fheil

d'fhéadfainn impí ar Hymenaeus
gan mé a threorú chun na bainise

d'fhéadfainn achainí air
a thóirse a mhúchadh

a fhir is a mhná dána a chur chun siúil
an fheis a chur ar ceal.

Ach fiú dá mbeadh a fhios agam é
táim dearfa go ndéarfainn

tabhair dom mo ghasúir
tabhair dom mo ghasúir ar ais nó ar éigean.

CELIA DE FRÉINE

Chalice of My Blood

Had I known
when I played in the schoolyard

my blood was not the same
as that of other girls

my body was still
nourished by foreign blood

I could have prayed
this chalice be taken from me

I could have promised myself
before falling in love

to lure the man of my choice
through hospital maze

to find out whether we were suited
and if not

I could have begged Hymenaeus
not to lead me to the altar

I could have entreated him
to quench his torch

dismiss his minstrels
cancel the feast.

But even had I known
I'm sure I would have said

give me my children
give me my children whatever the cost.

– translation of 'Cailís mo Chuid Fola' by the author

EAVAN BOLAND

Quarantine

In the worst hour of the worst season
  of the worst year of a whole people
a man set out from the workhouse with his wife.
He was walking – they were both walking – north.

She was sick with famine fever and could not keep up.
  He lifted her and put her on his back.
He walked like that west and west and north.
Until at nightfall under freezing stars they arrived.

In the morning they were both found dead.
  Of cold. Of hunger. Of the toxins of a whole history.
But her feet were held against his breastbone.
The last heat of his flesh was his last gift to her.

Let no love poem ever come to this threshold.
  There is no place here for the inexact
praise of the easy graces and sensuality of the body.
There is only time for this merciless inventory:

Their death together in the winter of 1847.
  Also what they suffered. How they lived.
And what there is between a man and woman.
And in which darkness it can best be proved.

GRACE WILENTZ

Dear Doctor Gold

"On the phone we spoke about the CAT scan report
and its failure to identify the hepatic lobe lesions –

    I think this is an unacceptable oversight
and want to have the CAT scan reviewed regarding the situation
    in the liver.

I may have gone through chemotherapy without much trouble,
    but these CAT scans are hard for me.
To think no one even bothered
    to follow through in reading the results
    is disheartening.

I have a CAT scan coming up in mid November
    and an appointment with you then
    on the 20th.
I want to make sure I get the most out of this scan.
    For instance, I would like
to have my uterus checked out,
also my bone density.
    Can the CAT scan look at these things?

Could you please make sure
    they look carefully at everything
    (lung, liver, etc)
and at uterus and fibroids and bones if appropriate?

    Could someone call me to say you got this?"

WILLIAM WORDSWORTH

Old Man Travelling

The little hedge-row birds,
That peck along the road, regard him not.
He travels on, and in his face, his step,
His gait, is one expression; every limb,
His look and bending figure, all bespeak
A man who does not move with pain, but moves
With thought – He is insensibly subdued
To settled quiet: he is one by whom
All effort seems forgotten, one to whom
Long patience has such mild composure given,
That patience now doth seem a thing, of which
He hath no need. He is by nature led
To peace so perfect, that the young behold
With envy, what the old man hardly feels.
 – I asked him whither he was bound, and what
The object of his journey; he replied
"Sir! I am going many miles to take
A last leave of my son, a mariner,
Who from a sea-fight has been brought to Falmouth,
And there is dying in a hospital."

Rainbow Blood

Somewhere over the rainbow,
The night continues underground;
The gays are meeting for drinks in bars designed for
    just them, and men with gentle knuckles,
Because we're still scared.

Somewhere over the rainbow,
Drag queens cram into tight spaces -
There's safety in the number of people you don't have to
    explain your love to,
Because we're still scared.

Somewhere over the rainbow,
All of Dorothy's friends have come down from the high
    the mighty propped us up on.
We've packed up and pocketed the streamers from the
    day of celebration gone.
Because we're still scared.

Somewhere over the rainbow,
Avoiding violet bruises and bloody lips,
We find the tribes we Belong To and make families of
    queer friends,

Because we're still scared.
Of Bleeding Rainbow Blood.

TARA BERGIN

Restriction

There has been this feeling,
of restriction.
In the hands especially –
So much so
I think of them as bandaged.
I think of them as motionless,
polite,
and resting on the table,
at a distance, as it were.
And all this time I am busy.
I call up whole boats,
whole fish, whole houses,
but they get added to a list
of things to do
when I can use my hands.
I get breathless climbing,
thinking up whole men,
whole women, and I
add them to the list.
I get breathless standing:
whole hawthorns, whole ash trees,
and I add these also.
I try to understand
why I feel this way,
why I have this feeling
of restriction in the hands.

I dream of my hands:
they shock me with what they do.
I try to understand
why I dream these things.
I call up a whole future.
I add it to the list.

SEÁN Ó RÍORDÁIN

Fiabhras

Tá sléibhte na leapa mós ard,
Tá breoiteacht 'na brothall 'na lár,
Is fada an t-aistear urlár,
    Is na mílte is na mílte i gcéin
    Tá suí agus seasamh sa saol.

Atáimid i gceantar bráillín,
Ar éigean más cuimhin linn cathaoir,
Ach bhí tráth sar ba mhachaire sinn,
    In aimsir choisíochta fadó,
    Go mbímis chomh hard le fuinneog.

Tá pictiúir ar an bhfalla ag at,
Tá an fráma imithe ina lacht,
Ceal creidimh ní féidir é bhac,
    Tá nithe ag druidim fém dhéin,
    Is braithim ag titum an saol.

Tá ceantar ag taisteal ón spéir,
Tá comharsanacht suite ar mo mhéar,
Dob fhuirist dom breith ar shéipéal,
    Tá ba ar an mbóthar ó thuaidh,
    Is níl ba na síoraíochta chomh ciúin.

Fever

It's a steep climb from the bed.
The sickly sweltering mound
is a long way from the ground.
Miles and miles away
folks still sit and stand.

We're here in the terrain of sheets.
We can barely recall a chair.
Once we stood sound on level ground,
in a time of walking, long ago.
We stood as tall as the window.

A picture swells off the wall.
The frame melts into a haze.
Reason can't stop it.
Things close in around me,
the dizzy world spins apart.

A locality is forming in the ether,
a parish perches on my finger.
I could easily pluck off a chapel.
There are cows on the road to the north.
The cows of eternity are not as tranquil.

– translation of 'Fiabhras' by **Greg Delanty**

MOLLY TWOMEY

Babysitter

When I was swapping Coco Pops
for low-fat cottage cheese,

saving up for an ab belt
and pleading with God to sculpt me thin,

my babysitter showed me
an ad on TV of children

with swollen abdomens and fruit flies
in the corners of their crusting lips.

These kids, she said, *would give anything*
for the chicken dippers under your plate,

the Penguin bar tucked up your sleeve.
After that everything tasted like guilt

but still I gripped the trophy of my ribs,
refused each sugared drink.

She was the first to see what I was becoming
and not praise me for it.

PAMELA GILLILAN

Menopause

Moods' ebb and flow ruled
by bright or clouded days,
not by the forceful womb.

Belly will not grow round again
unless, like a man's, from excess;
but not unsexed, not done with love.

Invisibly new-seasoned.
Long vassaldom served through.
Self, while the light lasts.

BOB HICOK

Her My Body

The dog licks my hand as I worry
about the left nipple
of the woman in the bathroom.

She is drying her hair, the woman
whose left nipple is sore.
We looked this evening
for diagonal cuts
or discolouration
or bite marks from small insects
that may be in our bed.

It is a good bed, a faithful bed.
A bed that won't be hurt
by the consideration we gave
to the possibility of small
though disproportionately
strong insects in our bed.

The blow dryer sounds like a jet
taking off. The first time
I flew to Brussels, people began
the journey happy but ended
with drool on their shirts.

She is drying her hair
though she has never been to Brussels.

Drying her hair
though she could be petting a dog.
Drying her hair
while having red thoughts
about what the pain in her nipple means.

I would not dry my hair
in such a moment but I am bald.
The body of the woman
has many ways to cease
being the body of the woman.

I have one way
to be happy
and she is that way.

I would like to fly with her to Brussels.
We would not be put off by the drool.
This is what happens when people sleep.
We would buy postcards of the little boy
who saved Brussels when he peed on a fire.
We would be romantic in public places.

For the moment
these desires can best be furthered
by petting a dog.

I'm also working on this theory.
That sometimes a part of the body
just hurts.

That the purpose of prayer
is to make the part of the body
that sometimes just hurts
the little toe or appendix.

Something vestigial or redundant.
Something that can be jettisoned.

I have no reason
to use the word cancer
while petting a dog.

There is a piece of a second
during which a jet is not flying
nor is it on the ground.

I'm working on a theory
that no one can die
inside that piece of a second.

If you are comforted
by this thought you are welcome
to keep it.

GERARD SMYTH

Daytime Sleeper

Curtain cloth
blindfolds the house.
Hands of the clock
move forward
with feebler and feebler effort.
The chimes are wearying
at noon and midnight.

The pillow,
white for tranquillity,
has been warmed
by sun that shines
too little or too much.

In the room
of the daytime sleeper
the struggle against sleep
waxes and wanes.
Flowers grieve
for their lost fragrance.
Bluebottles round
uneaten fruit
are giddy with impatience.

VONA GROARKE

Returning from Illness

(an ordinary illness)
as if I'd had my head in the freezer
for a matter of some hours and had seen
(by which I mean cornea, iris. All that.)
a future so stern and bare and cold
I could look only at its black rim
(the ruthless calm, the ice and certainty),

those hours dissolved the heat of my skin,
one and another and another still
all gone, nothing to show for them

but damp sheets and the pillow too
which I, even in fever, had swapped,
to believe a clean start possible
or, if not possible, mine.

And thought recovering from illness
much like returning from love:
the same habit of having to say,
Yes, this is my body: I will live in it.

TRACY K. SMITH

In Your Condition

That whole time away, I stayed dizzy. Everywhere,
Meats whirled round in a pit. Waiters crashed in
And out like the tide with trays and trays of fish.
Every chance, I slept: in the bathroom between courses,
A whole half-hour laid out like a corpse atop the bed.
I saw the beach from a castle in the hills. I climbed there
On Sunday carrying my purse, snapping the same pictures
From the year before, to be polite. Windows that belonged
To the queen maintain their perfect shape, though the glass
She would have paced behind is gone. Grass spreads
Like intrigue where once were rugs, and a double metal rail
Suggests a wall. Along a hall and up slick winding steps,
There was a view down into the valley, but I couldn't linger.
The baby kept me queasy, hungry, made my dress hike up
Though I was only eight weeks in. At a tavern on my last night,
I had to stand outside to breathe. I ordered bottle after bottle
Of water, though the red wine shimmered like nectar.
Flying home, I snuck a wedge of brie, and wept
Through a movie starring Angelina Jolie.

COLM TÓIBÍN

Two Plus One

My heart is watching and weakening
Mercilessly counting the beats;
It is bored, casually waiting
For this to cease.

My father died at fifty-three.
Vessels leaked in his brain.
Then arteries weakened.
He moaned in pain.

My mother's eyes were grey as his
Were blue. Her breath
Rose high over the town
Before it sank in death.

I have their two weak hearts in one
Weak heart, their eyes merged in my gaze.
His slow smile, her soft side-glance
Oversee my days.

MARK ROPER

Colonoscope

The tiny camera travels
down memory lane.

Finds, in the folds of my colon,
the hands of my fathers,

painted so long ago
on the walls of the cave.

The ancestral grip,
the hold they have on me.

The blueprint my body
is primed to follow.

Finds, in the cell's obedience,
the son's obedience.

ÁINE NÍ GHLINN

Cuair

Ó ghoid máinlia
a banúlacht uaithi
bíonn sí de shíor
ag stándadh
ar éirí na gréine
ar chomhchruinneas na gnoc.

Ar pháipéar déanann
stuanna ciorcail
ceann i ndiaidh a chéile.

Ó fágadh coilm sceanna
mar a mbíodh a brollach
tá sí ciaptha ag cuair.

ÁINE NÍ GHLINN

Curves

Since a surgeon
stole her femininity
she stares constantly
at the rising sun
at the roundness of hills.

On paper she draws
arcs of circles
circle after circle.
Since a scar
replaced her breast
she is tortured by curves.

– translation of 'Cuair' by the author

CAITRÍONA O'REILLY

X-Ray

A vertical chain of spine:
flesh cloaks the bones'
articulation in shadow.
The Tree of Life, but not
of Knowledge: shot through
with this god's radiance, light
shook from his metallic hair,
the gravity of his glance
decreeing me unscrolled
as the killer might decipher
his victim, delicately
parting the belly's vellum.
I am lain against the plate
and dazzled: the light inimical,
the weight that enters weightless.
A thrown shadow dissects
the self from what it was.
Can flesh become all shadow?
Not yet: as through a glass
brightly and fragile as a bird's
shine my long blue bones.

WILLIAM KEOHANE

Top Surgery

Two lines of light, wounds
open

the past drops out – a cluster
of red stars –

from my chest and onto
the table; metal instruments
latex vinyl wrapped trained hands, mopped brows, pie
slices of artificial brightness above. I look

down at the flat plain, new
man.

And ask the air: *is this mine?*
all of it – every inch of scar and –
Yes
the voice carrying me says. *This is your chest.*

RITA ANN HIGGINS

Philomena's Revenge

As a teenager
she was like any other,
boys, the craic,
smoking down the backs.

Later there was talk
she broke things,
furniture and glass,
her mother's heart.

"Mad at the world,"
the old women nod
round each other's faces.

But it was more
than that
and for less
she was punished.

That weekend
she didn't leave a cup alone
every chair hit the wall,
Philomena's revenge.

Soon after
she was shifted
and given the shocks.

Round each other's faces
the old women nod,
"Treatment, treatment
they've given her the treatment."

These days
she gets on with the furniture,
wears someone else's walk,
sees visions in glass.

She's good too
for getting the messages;
small things, bread and milk
sometimes the paper,

and closing the gate
after her father drives out,
she waits for his signal
he always shouts twice,

"Get the gate Philo,
get the gate, girl."

DAMIAN SMYTH

The Killard Emergency Room

On these sands, it is always autumn and dusk;
And constantly lit like an asylum or orphanage,
An underground; everywhere magnolia, an orangerie
Of strange concerns and quiet action, a place best avoided;
Pale slopes, several rooms, and somewhere the sea
As subdued as the voices are, carried on warm air.
There are beachcombers alright who already are things
And nothing else – that trick of the light or the camber
Which makes monsters of children and old men of wrack.
They are busy gathering tinder from twigs in my chest,
Entering through what's still the soft underbelly of Europe –
The Dardanelles, Gallipoli, the Hellespont, Crimea –
Postcards from the shell-shocked strays arriving in the town.
The chap holding my hand is, in fact, gliding
A sliver of light the full length of an artery; eventually,
I'm lit up like a delta that vessels are plying – silverfish, salmon;
Light playing the dunes as if someone was overboard;
Pink sails suddenly and the muttering of an engine;
Torches making cave walls shake; a name called out in the fog.
The tide the open gown lets loose has a body in it.

ZOË BRIGLEY

Infertility

Doctors have their ways to investigate: microscope eyes
that count the glittering fish of sperm, cameras that stalk
beaded eyes into the gorgeous-red heart of the cervix.
The ultrasound wand probes, presses, sucks to measure the orb
of each egg in its sac, while x-rays unravel the womb,
a stretched concertina that spasms even as it fills
with saline. Later there's chemical mingling of your blood
and mine, to map how XY arms and legs of chromosomes
embrace or fist. Here I am in the stark, unforgiving
sonographer's light: a passage, narrow key, squat cave
gorged by blood, or just a ripening plum with arid seeds.
Here am I, a woman not a body, in the snowlight
outside the hospital, where I smear the whitened sidewalk
and run with my long legs, my pretty body still unveined,
still to be spoiled by the loving-soft fat of motherhood.
So many women come to me saying, "I have lost too,
and this one, and this one." So many embryos retreat
to flesh: the live cell of the mother. Don't tell me that it
will happen for me, when the only sure thing is a miracle:
the sperm nuzzling in its nest and the egg that opens, explodes.

ELEANOR HOOKER

Tamponade

our hearts on a heavy chain
fastened to a faithful rib ...
— Vasko Popa

Still and light she lies,
all eight years of her,
her lips stained blue,
as though she's feasted
on summer berries.
And when the pressure
falls inside her lungs
it builds in the powered
bellows breathing into her.
And when you listen,
you hear only a muffled heart.

You are the crash team
assembled round her bed,
who watch the surgeon cut
into the space
above her fifth rib,
to remove a clot,
who tells you to place
your gloved hand
round her heart.

You hear his *dear God,*
and think of 'the God' hung
in your grandmother's parlour –
sorrowful and kitsch, gaping,
heart in hand –
sac-red, barbed and glowing.

And with this ultimate
transgression, tiny heart in hand,
its critical defences breached,
you repeat the child's name,
Faith, Faith –
You do not pray,
you speak homing words
to her bird-spirit,
that hovers, heartsore.

Note: *Tamponade, compression of the heart by an
accumulation of fluid in the pericardial sac.*

STEPHANIE CONN

Cross-Section with Contrast

They are scanning the inside of my body –
abdominal cavity, blood vessels, bones.
Iodine pulses through my veins, flushes warm
and wet between my legs. I've been forewarned,
assured I will not piss myself. A man with kind eyes
squeezes my hand, twice, then steps behind a screen.
I wonder if it's bullet proof. I'm on my back, stripped
of my wedding ring, the necklace from my daughters;
they hold no traction here, in this room of machines
that ignore the heart in favour of the stiller organs.

Blasted by a thousand suns

BERNARD O'DONOGHUE

Ter Conatus

Sister and brother, nearly sixty years
They'd farmed together, never touching once.
Of late she had been coping with a pain
In her back, realisation dawning slowly
That it grew differently from the warm ache
That resulted periodically
From heaving churns on to the milking-stand.

She wondered about the doctor. When,
Finally, she went, it was too late,
Even for chemotherapy. And still
She wouldn't have got round to telling him,
Except that one night, watching television,
It got so bad she gasped, and struggled up,
Holding her waist. "D'you want a hand?" he asked,

Taking a step towards her. "I can manage,"
She answered, feeling for the stairs.
Three times, like that, he tried to reach her.
But, being so little practised in such gestures,
Three times the hand fell back, and took its place,
Unmoving at his side. After the burial,
He let things take their course. The neighbours watched

In pity the rolled-up bales, standing
Silent in the fields, with the aftergrass
Growing into them, and wondered what he could
Be thinking of: which was that evening when,
Almost breaking with a lifetime of
Taking real things for shadows,
He might have embraced her with a brother's arms.

ANNE KENNEDY

In the Women's Cancer Ward

I – Breakfast

Across from me a Dublin woman
drops her spoon
milk spatters from her porridge,
"I can't use my hand –
soon I won't be able to tie
the ribbons in my daughter's hair."

The unseen child takes shape,
silky ribbons bobbing
the mother's breast heaves
beneath her bargain pearls.

II – Waiting for Treatment

We're targeted for treatment
red noughts and crosses
quilting our skin.
The young woman who knits
acts unperturbed.
"I'm barely scratched," she tells us,
"They just removed the lump.
Early stage –
I don't really need radiation."

Her needles click,
she drops a stitch.

A woman from Donegal says,
"He cut me from the shoulder
to the waist.
Old-style surgeon,
did I jump the gun?
Someone suggested a second opinion."

She kneads her hands
rolling invisible dough
then stares down at the floor.
No one speaks.

III – Watching the News

Wearing her leather money-belt
like a bandolier,
her painful tongue and gums
have betrayed her.
Still the Sergeant Major barks orders:
"Switch the Channels."

She doesn't want news from the Republic,
not even from Ulster.
She colonises the day room
mounts surveillance on the TV
subjects us all to nasal
static from the BBC.

IV – The Royal Wedding

In the day room
Diana's veil fills the screen,
her smile stretches from London
to Ballymun.
Death watches in a pink jumper,
chain-smoking.

Vows professed,
the straight-backed chairs
empty their tired occupants,
ruined breasts, lost wombs
into the hot July afternoon.

V – The Young Bride

The young bride lies outside her covers
wearing a white blouse.
Buds inside her breasts scatter their seeds
down her spine.
They float in the furrows
of her bones.

On our daily walk she moves
carefully, becoming a shadow
under the flashing canopy of trees.

At the end of the avenue
she asks to turn back, explaining,
"My husband will be here at 4."
She buys him chocolate from the hospital kiosk,
I link her on the lawn.

VI – Blurred Vision

At tea time I peel an orange
for the woman with the eye patch,
her vision is blurred.

She tells me of her caravan in Clare
where she'll be going for the summer,
of her children
singing in the sand
and a husband who will be her eyes.

The long twilight tints the bedclothes,
her time is short
yet summer stretches on forever.

VII – Raspberries in Rathgar

Each evening after treatment
I walk slowly into Rathgar
to buy baskets full of nippled berries.
I can't get enough of them,
their ruby juice runs down my chin.

More than swallows,
raspberries make a summer,
their season so short
so delicious,
shop fronts full of punnets.
Buying raspberries,
I'm running in a race I cannot win.

VIII – The Night Nurse

Pushing night's trolley through the pneumatic hush,
back and neck erect,
caryatid with silver braids,
veins twine the pillars of her legs.
3 a.m., cradles the insomniac whispering,
"My dear, sleeping pills don't suit you,
we'll throw them all away."

Will my blood, scoured with mustard gas,
hermetically blasted by a thousand suns
flow pure again and strong?
And will the weekend
when I see my children
ever come?

RAYMOND CARVER

What the Doctor Said

He said it doesn't look good
he said it looks bad in fact real bad
he said I counted thirty-two of them on one lung before
I quit counting them
I said I'm glad I wouldn't want to know
about any more being there than that
he said are you a religious man do you kneel down
in forest groves and let yourself ask for help
when you come to a waterfall
mist blowing against your face and arms
do you stop and ask for understanding at those moments
I said not yet but I intend to start today
he said I'm real sorry he said
I wish I had some other kind of news to give you
I said Amen and he said something else
I didn't catch and not knowing what else to do
and not wanting him to have to repeat it
and me to have to fully digest it
I just looked at him
for a minute and he looked back it was then
I jumped up and shook hands with this man who'd just given me
something no one else on earth had ever given me
I may even have thanked him habit being so strong

STEPHEN SEXTON

Valley Fortress

These are the days of no letters her signature starved with jitters
in the few half hours she's awake to make arrangements:
            no flowers
no more than is natural for a swift discreet funeral
and burial with her parents tea and sandwiches afterwards.
She sleeps the undertaker leaves the fountain leaks in
            the courtyard.
My head is heavier than stone. I read yesterday's newspapers
eat crisps from the vending machine I want to die is what she says
not either asleep or awake let me please die is what she says.
It's me I'm here is what I say but I am not since she is not.
Then she says I want to go home once more for one once more
            one night
and I say you can't go home now she says I know not now after.

SHIRLEY McCLURE

The Argument for Chemotherapy

Imagine we wanted
to knock down this wall,
says the doctor.
This pen is the hammer,
which represents the tablets.

And he begins to
tap tap tap
with his ball-point pen
on the cool white wall
beside his desk.

I wonder who's next door,
an intern with a headache
or another imagistic doctor,
rapping for *her* patients' benefit
on the opposite side,

till one day,
many demonstrations
down the road,
a keyhole of hope
is exposed.

Eventually,
he rests his silver biro
on my case notes, *we would*
break down the wall.
But what if, and he stands,

I took a sledgehammer?
He swipes with tailored jacket arms,
a Victorian High Striker, a Thor:
Now you see what happens
to the wall?

FRANK ORMSBY

McQuade

When McQuade went up for a ball
He came down with snow on his heels,
And when McQuade took a shot the goalie
Had to hitch-hike back to the field:
A legend from the tall decades behind,
Like 'Bawler' Donnelly and the Night of the Big Wind.

A quiet cancer stopped him, its tackle sly,
Decisive. Shocked, I watched him fall,
Saw Death collect him, easily as a loose ball.

JANE CLARKE

Metastasis

The way couch grass takes hold of a garden,
spreads seeds, runners, white rhizomes
long before we notice, the way it grows

more tenacious when we begin to dig,
gathering different names – dog grass,
scutch grass, quick grass, twitch grass,

the way it creeps along the ground,
then sends a root deep down,
slips silent under fences, colonises beds

and gets itself entangled through agapanthus
Midnight Blue, the way that it persists,
the way that it persists.

DAVID WHEATLEY

Despair

after Seán Ó Ríordáin

No dead men will leave the tomb
to seek out the confines of night or day.
Abandon your designs on them
and humble your bare head to the clay.

Don't think you can put flesh on a wraith.
The beautiful was never true.
I know that My Redeemer lieth.
No pennies will fall from heaven for you.

You want a pooka to breathe down your neck,
and all the heavenly lies he'd spin.
You've settled for the hump on your back:
don't let it spread to the brain.

Amidst your pooka shadowmancy
find the pooka truth and way.
Cast a hunchshadow all can see
and humble your bare head to the clay.

Make a show of yourself. The critic rates
the hunchshadowself you hide in
that once was laid between the sheets
to kiss while deafness blew from heaven.

And a gentle hand entombed and rotting,
a dream in a separate tomb imprisoned,
the dearest dream, the rarest thing,
in a deep tomb inside the mind,

and the black chalice of night drained low,
and a crooked sleep, tossed left and right,
while Veronica mopped His brow,
while the hunchback stripped bare in the night.

Hypocrite lecteur who read
the poem I beget on sickness,
try judging *that* and then decide
what is failure and what success.

JAMES O'LEARY

Holding Joe

In a locked ward with safe surfaces,
we are sitting still in the visiting room
when you tell me you tried it again –
this morning – between room checks.

We are sitting, still in the visiting room.
I look at the soft-rubber coat hooks.
This morning, between room checks,
you nearly succeeded.

I look at the soft-rubber coat hooks
and quietly ask how you did it.
You nearly succeeded.
I don't know what to do for you

and quietly ask how you did it
when you tell me you tried it again.
I don't know what to do for you
in a locked ward with safe surfaces.

GERALDINE MITCHELL

Cephalalgia

I am obsessed with all things cerebral,
that is to say, anything
resembling a brain – reeled

into folds, folded into crevices,
I dream of ruched camisoles,
winding cloths, swaddles and shrouds.

I have developed a kitten's weakness for wool,
balls that unspool into labyrinths,
an attraction to circuit boards,

tangles of fishing line, coiled snakes and
smoke rings, worm casts at
low tide, cephalopod molluscs, the cochlea

in each of my cat's ears
– all because
the walnut lodged in my skull

will not surrender the ink-soaked
husk that hugs the grooved shell
that shelters the membrane that papers

the twin hemispheres
that make up the soft part,
the sore heart of my head.

MAURICE RIORDAN

The Cranium

after Neruda

I didn't give it a thought until I was knocked down
and I heard my soul roll away in the dark.

I was dead to the world, gone – but then pain,
a spasm, and the throbbing flare of blue lights.

Later, I could pick out the moonscape of the ward,
between sleeps that felt like dirty cotton wool.

This morning my hand extended a shaky finger,
poking at the cuts and bruises, until it found

one item still whole, still game: you, poor skull –
how vainly across the years, hustling, on the prowl,

I'd examine every hair, check over each feature,
but miss the prime asset – your handsome dome

enclosing the delicate wetware of vessels
and pathways, the impossibly knotted connectors,

all that softly booming vegetal chemistry
a mini-ocean into which reason shoots bright bolts

and where, among sea-wrack and fronds of childhood,
the fish of volition darts now here, now there ...

Where too, who knows, my timid soul hides out.
Tap-tap, knock-knock! Adam, wakey-wakey!

I'm the stonecutter on the hillside stripped clean
of trees and birdsong bowing to the trusty marble.

Or a safecracker on his knees in a vault, his ear
to the steel door, trembling for it to open.

PÁDRAIG J. DALY

Alzheimer's

for Frank

Seeing you as you are
Unnerves me,
All that you were
Evaporated.

Where does your mind wander now?
Does it wake ever,
Welcoming us to the door
Of that ramshackle house in Inchicore,

Leading us through the hall,
Urging us to watch the step,
Opening the whiskey with a twist,
Calling down to your wife in the kitchen?

And how do you remember her?
Her mirth? Her tenderness? Her thousand vendettas?
Will we never again listen
To you chuckle through your yarns –

The girl in your bedroom in France,
Making your boss gasp at your worldliness?
The friend from Cork
Reinventing himself with Trinity intonation?

How does the blank that keeps your features link
With the glory that was you?

PAUL DURCAN

The Head Transplant

The doctor said to me: Your father needs a *new* head.
So I said to the doctor: You can give him *my* head.

My days were numbered – broken marriage, cancer,
False teeth, bad dreams – so "Yes" was his answer.

Now I lie in my bed wondering away in my head
What will my father look like with his new head?

Will he look like a bull with the head of a daffodil
Or like a nonagenarian pontiff with the head of a harlot?

Or like a heavyweight weightlifter with the head of a fox
Or like a withered, agèd, tree with the sun in its branches?

My dreams and memories will percolate down his legs and arms;
My ideas will seep down his spine like the roots of a tree.

And my eyes will swivel in obeisance to their new rotator.
His friends will say: "Quite remarkable the change in Old Johnny –

His new head seems to be doing him the world of good.
Jolly lucky that blackguard son of his snuffed it when he did."

And I, when I'm dead, will walk alone in the graveyard,
A ghost with no head, an authentic hobgoblin.

A truly real Irishman, a *giolla gan ceann*.

EOIN DEVEREUX

The Bullfield

On All Souls' Day
I knelt down on the mottled Tundra clay.
Ear cupped to the frozen ground,
I could faintly hear
the murmurings of men
buried, nameless in the paupers' grave.

Simple men like Francie Murphy and Brendan Plunkett,
let out for the day,
to belly crawl over damp drills,
handpicking potatoes, Greyhound Cabbage, carrots, turnips, mangles.
It takes a lot of work to feed a hospital.

In the Bullfield,
I see Mattie Keane and Pa O'Brien,
able-bodied innocents,
chopping wood or ricking turf,
thrown the odd Players or Woodbine
as payment for their toil.

In the Bullfield,
I see tormented men like Jim Sullivan and Dinny Ryan,
fattening pigs with sour milk and potato skins,
slopping out greeny brown scutter from their pens.

I see them all, and somehow cannot deny them,
men who were dumped in silence at first light,
from the back of a blue Ford tractor,
exchanging their labour,
for bed and board,
in the madhouse, named after
the Patron Saint of Workers.

RACHEL HANDLEY

Remembrance

In my dream you were alive. I said I
loved you and you heard me. You knew it was
me, not just distance with a human shape.
You tell me I need to stay here, so I
do. I grab the thread of sewn pink petals
hanging tight between us, their wet edges
drip your soft thunder all over the floor,
liquid velvet slips between our fingers,
soaked; we campaign to walk against time. Come
see me, you said, before I forget. You
knew, before we knew, that the dementia
was slithering in, knocking out pieces
of you with its blunt mouth. I'd put you back
together if I could, click each petal
into its stem so that I could say I
love you and you could hear me.

TERRY McDONAGH

In The End ...

maybe it was your picture
of a boatman on the lake

and the shadow of a child
along an autumn horizon

that made me look inwards
and not out to the galaxies

where dreams are stars –
eclipses are closer to home.

I need more twilight now
to shut down on bustle, and

a place to lie down with kin
next to an open window.

DENNIS O'DRISCOLL

Admissions

Before you do down life again,
badmouth a world that never lives up
to its billing, recall how glorious it seemed,
your unwillingness to let go, that evening
you were driven to Admissions.

Every shabby sight you passed
gleamed with some ameliorating
feature, mustering enough initiative
to demonstrate its best case scenario.
Your own scrawny excuse for a lawn –

one part weed to two parts moss –
glowed with previously unsuspected
zest; the day's remaining light was fraying
at the edges as the sun signed off on
the horizon's dotted line: a virtuosic chef,

concocting dishes from leftovers,
drizzling pigment, tossing in whatever
mix of clashing tinctures lay unused.
How carefree everyone appeared as
they flashed momentarily into view

along your painful route: tourists perusing
the early-bird menu, a buggy-wheeling
mother cutting through church grounds,
hoodies ganging up against the counter
in the steamy comfort of the takeaway.

That you fell for the world's seductive looks
that evening in the psychedelic dusk
is not to be denied; how some confidence –
insider information you had withheld until then –
was let slip: *and he saw that it was good.*

GERARD DONOVAN

Anniversary: To a Father

No more Mozart at two a.m.,
no more strings from cigarettes waved above a tuning finger
    on the radio dial,
no more static from Moscow, Berlin, London,
voices scoured from the steel grid
to give the ghostly smoke a sound,
no more arguments at midnight over nothing I can remember now,
no more silences spread and read like a newspaper,
no more debates after a night's drink over bread and butter,
no more bedside paperbacks of Sophocles, Aristotle, de Chardin,
who brought forth nothing but more mystery,
no more forgiveness after years of silence.

I have been reading Donne again.
A month ago, driving westward on Long Island,
I faced the evening sun
thinking that the circle resting was the left eye of a woman
whose other opened out of sight in permanent night
as she lay on her side, always in two worlds,
rinsed in the blue and orange sheets of dusk's slant,
and that if I followed in twilight long enough,
she would rise to meet me
from a golden morning on blowing sea-drenched sheets.

You went without a warning bell
or calls to come quickly, no airports,
running along antiseptic corridors,
torturing time out of waiting rooms.
The nurses said you laughed and then slumped.
We came after the grim news –
numb that a spirit could leave with such ease
the body it chafed against for seventy years;
I stood like a child fooled out of pain by a practised doctor
who rips the bandage off at the wrong count.
Tonight I try to remove whatever sticks to my skin –
I peel hair by hair, hoping a wound remade will prove
that separation itself is the proper act of remembering.

To die at the right time: words easier understood than said.
A second manufactured on either side for comfort
brings no balance, no safe passage;
in that space crowd monsters without name.

Old man, you cheated burial its journey
and the buriers their one metaphor:
this very night, one year later,
you lie on a slab in the university,
your body for science.
You went without the spells and the frightened scenery;

the curtains parted and your eyes shut
and the breath stopped in you
on that last line you delivered into the light: *Find me.*
Even with the best instruments
they'll come to nothing but a limp and a third of a lung;
no evidence of that philosopher
who went hunting in Rabbitt's bar
armed with a pint and an argument.

You went alone,
friends a finger-click away in the hall.
A year later you come to me on a bus by a cliff in Morocco,
and as in life I have no words until you disappear.
Perhaps this poem is nothing more than a dial I turn
   to hear you again.
Nothing. These words conjure no voice but last words
and no vista but words;
and the woman will never rise. Her dawn eye
watches small boats drift from harbours
on the other side of the world.

From underground springs
and pure enough to drink

ANNEMARIE NÍ CHURREÁIN

Bog Medicine

Drink these star-leafed nettles
and keep in your purse a fern.

To become invisible, say your harm
to the hill.

This hill is pagan.
This hill is Hill.

It will answer in bog-tongue
and occasional fire,
burning back the earth
along the heather-stream

despite bald heels of rock,
despite the kissy mink,
despite a saintly air

until the stream runs dark
with what needs
to blacken out of you.

SIOBHÁN CAMPBELL

Doctor Verse

This is how I will approach it,
like a man, clipped and sure
and partisan. Establish
the problem, identify the cause,
then possibly prescribe a ream
of love, of exile or of loss.

But what is a love poem now?
An affirmation within which
hope can grow, a faith we've
forgotten how to speak
that things, all manner of things,
can be well even though
we've shut the gate of hell?

Did we know when we gave up
being redeemed how it would feel
out here on the slopes where
literature is frozen in its tracks –
no beckoning heights, nothing below,
only an ice-laden sky and the careless
tumble of snow?

GAIL McCONNELL

Octopus

Panicked, with inky melanin
you make a slipstream to get free
or make autonomy an art

rewriting your anatomy.
Camouflage has failed, mimicry
cannot hold off attack. Scoring

your arms with incisions those claws.
Whose cuts are these? Who bruises, chews
at your skin, initiates this

severing? You watch it detach,
float away from you. Coppered blood
infuses the already blue.

Self-sabotage, the first and last
stage of collage, the cutting up
without the glue. The bitten limb

goes unattached, but is renewed.
You didn't know you knew the art
of self-repair until alone

those hundred days, watching something
grow. New cups bloom the length of you;
mouths opening by small degrees.

The whipping fins can be withstood,
the gripping jaws. All that issues
from the deep, in all likelihood.

NITHY KASA

The Herbalist

There once was a man,
who knew each tree by name.
A forest whisperer, he would lay an ear
like a stethoscope against the trunks,
as if there were heartbeats to hear,
and called the barks SKIN.
He spoke fluent forestry,
and knew forest elements:
the scents of the floras,
each bird's cry.
Planted lemon grass for tea,
bitter leaf for malaria,
the wizard had potions for the cursed
who lost their minds.
He chewed kola nuts like candy,
the crunch of the pungent seeds
crushing in his mouth, audible,
where all hailed him from a distance.
The siblings from the next croft,
who kept us company, had told us
of how they carried their father to the herbalist
when a snake had bitten him,
almost dropping him on the way.
They played out how my grandfather
tucked in their father like a child.

The poor with their medieval sicknesses,
were left on their own
when the herbalist was gone.
And you couldn't take it,
watching him swallow pills
from the man with the white coat.
I wondered then why he couldn't help himself,
him who healed a village.
It doesn't work that way.
The man who lived amongst the trees,
he, himself was a gem,
his eyelids were the lids of jugs, jars,
bottles, with herbal juices.
When his eyes closed,
they closed with him.

MICHAEL D. HIGGINS

The Well 2

To visit again the well of friendship,
And draw on the end of an old rope
The bucket of one's life,
To listen as it clatters
Against the sides,
Making a rattling resonance of childhood,
Is the stuff of pilgrimage.
To make the long haul back
For a sweet drink
From a decrepit vessel
Binds up time.
Water hidden under the earth emerges
And makes a renewal.
The deep drink forges an old unity
Beyond all uncertainty.

CHIAMAKA ENYI-AMADI

The Moon is a Healing Being

the moon is teaching me to heal the fear, of being and not being
seen the scourge, of many eyes or worse none at all lonely is
living without another being, next to me at all times breathing
without, another body to match the rise and, fall of my chest
some nights she surprises, me her face beaming with satisfaction,
a day well spent caring for her own self, she tells me just because
a person has, eyes doesn't mean they see you doesn't mean, they
would hold your hand through all your phases, each night the
sky is a firm silver chest, cradling her head basking in the blue,
of her glow full of gratitude for her, having come at last to keep
it company, bringing it laughter full to the belly, on some night's
she's worse off joy cut in half, needing to cry and go to bed early,
the moon is a healing being washing her, silver hair thankful
time is on her side, longing to lie her weary head on the, warm
cotton chest of her pillow not long, now till daybreak bringing a
damp cloth to, her aching arms and chest black soap kissing, the
soft dimples on her lower back shea, butter massaging her skin
soothing each, pore from toe to chin cherry balm sweet on, her
lips she cries she sings nothing is truly fixed not anger not fear not
even grief, she cools her sore eyes with fresh cucumber, slices her
bedtimes snack lavender, drops on trembling fingertips pressing,
into the nape of her neck the base of, her temples have stopped
ticking time is still, on her side as day breaks into a cold, sweat she
settles into sleep dreaming of, the distant sky knowing it will soon
light, up when it sees her rested smile beaming, over Dublin bay

THEO DORGAN

Skull of a Curlew

Skull of a curlew full of stars,
my mouth on fire with black, unspeakable bees.
Light on the lime boles, bleached and bare,
my gorge rising, crammed with blackfurred bees.

Clay of the orchard on my cheek,
cheeks puffed like wind on a map's margin.
Dust in each lungful of cold air,
lips burned on the inside by black bees.

> I wait for the moon to rise me
> I pray to the midnight ant
> I clutch at fistfuls of wet grass
> I hammer the earth with bare heels.

Skull of a curlew full of stars,
night sky dredged with the eyes of bees.
Black fire around each star,
I swallow fear in mouthfuls of fur and wing.

Skull of a curlew full of stars,
the great hive of heaven heavy around me.
I spit out bees and black anger,
mouth of a curlew, fountain of quiet stars.

SINÉAD MORRISSEY

& Forgive Us Our Trespasses

Of which the first is love. The sad, unrepeatable fact
That the loves we shouldn't foster burrow faster and linger longer
Than sanctioned kinds can. Loves that thrive on absence, on lack
Of return, or worse, on harm, are unkillable, Father.
They do not die in us. And you know how we've tried.
Loves nursed, inexplicably, on thoughts of sex,
A return to touched places, a backwards glance, a sigh –
They come back like the tide. They are with us at the terminus
When cancer catches us. They have never been away.
Forgive us the people we love – their dragnet influence.
Those disallowed to us, those who frighten us, those who stay
On uninvited in our lives and every night revisit us.
Accept from us the inappropriate
By which our dreams and daily scenes stay separate.

ELIZABETH BISHOP

The Man-Moth

Man-Moth: Newspaper misprint for 'mammoth'.

Here, above,
cracks in the buildings are filled with battered moonlight.
The whole shadow of Man is only as big as his hat.
It lies at his feet like a circle for a doll to stand on,
and he makes an inverted pin, the point magnetised to the moon.
He does not see the moon; he observes only her vast properties,
feeling the queer light on his hands, neither warm nor cold,
of a temperature impossible to record in thermometers.

But when the Man-Moth
pays his rare, although occasional, visits to the surface,
the moon looks rather different to him. He emerges
from an opening under the edge of one of the sidewalks
and nervously begins to scale the faces of the buildings.
He thinks the moon is a small hole at the top of the sky,
proving the sky quite useless for protection.
He trembles, but must investigate as high as he can climb.

Up the façades,
his shadow dragging like a photographer's cloth behind him
he climbs fearfully, thinking that this time he will manage
to push his small head through that round clean opening
and be forced through, as from a tube, in black scrolls on the light.
(Man, standing below him, has no such illusions.)
But what the Man-Moth fears most he must do, although
he fails, of course, and falls back scared but quite unhurt.

Then he returns
to the pale subways of cement he calls his home. He flits,
he flutters, and cannot get aboard the silent trains
fast enough to suit him. The doors close swiftly.
The Man-Moth always seats himself facing the wrong way
and the train starts at once at its full, terrible speed,
without a shift in gears or a gradation of any sort.
He cannot tell the rate at which he travels backwards.

Each night he must
be carried through artificial tunnels and dream recurrent dreams.
Just as the ties recur beneath his train, these underlie
his rushing brain. He does not dare look out the window,
for the third rail, the unbroken draught of poison,
runs there beside him. He regards it as a disease
he has inherited the susceptibility to. He has to keep
his hands in his pockets, as others must wear mufflers.

If you catch him,
hold up a flashlight to his eye. It's all dark pupil,
an entire night itself, whose haired horizon tightens
as he stares back, and closes up the eye. Then from the lids
one tear, his only possession, like the bee's sting, slips.
Slyly he palms it, and if you're not paying attention
he'll swallow it. However, if you watch, he'll hand it over,
cool as from underground springs and pure enough to drink.

ÓRFHLAITH FOYLE

Take it from the Spleen, Baby Doll

Take it from the spleen, Baby Doll,
The heart ain't no good
for hate or love.
It digs a hole it can't get out
and nothing grows
with all the misery it wants to
solve.
Take it from the spleen, Little Girl,
with your Emily Dickinson flair;
maybe find a man
and sit on a rose garland chair
or some bed
made erotic
yet sweet
– as if your innocence unwrapped
is all the food you need to eat.
Take it from the spleen – you tell him,
little sister,
the heart just pumps it steady.
While the spleen
– oh my the spleen
oh my the spleen
– it gets you ready.

JEAN O'BRIEN

The Cure

As the mist lifts off the fields in the morning,
droplets dry in the air and sparkle
with white water that edges the tide.
As the sea retreats rock pools are exposed,
blue/black clams, tiny orange crabs,
white scalloped shells.
Cup it with your eyes and drink it in.

That last night beside me you cried out
in sleep. "Bastards. Bastards,"
with a venom that belied your daytime face.
Then I saw in your eyes
where too much light has been.
We sit together now, sandpaper people
scratching each other down to bone.

Just before nightfall go down to Spanish Point
and listen, listen to the wash thundering
the rocks. Hear the dark cormorants rustle
among seaweed and hear the long grasses
sigh and settle. Lie and listen until you reach
silence and the demons stop needling
your skin. Don't come in
near the city until you are quiet.

PAULA MEEHAN

One Evening in May

The sultry lead and pewter sky
opened on blue immensity
which hung a moment,
then sultry lead and pewter sky

clanged back. I thought I was wise
till I heard her voice; thought
I had the art of mirror plumbing
perfected. Then she showed me

in a blue clearing of clouds
how space can enrapture a mortal.
That small glimpse was worth
all the age's talk in the academies.

Since, I have wandered in a daze
imagining her everywhere, even
in the faces of the sick and damaged.
It's just her style to trick about

shapechanging all the while.
Whatever happens now, I'll be bound
to her rule for life. I pray I'll not rue
the day she parted clouds,

revealed her starry body, her great
snakeshead, her myriad children
feasting at her breasts. She spoke. She said,
"You're mine. Come. Do my bidding."

IMTIAZ DHARKER

Crab-Apples

My mother picked crab-apples
off the Glasgow apple trees
and pounded them with chillies
to change
her homesickness
into green chutney.

SEÁN HEWITT

St John's Wort

Named for a man who carries his own head
on a platter, for a day when the sun bears
its light over the land so slowly, so measuredly,
that the night crouches back and waits. A token
of love, of patience, of the will to lift the mind
outside oneself, and let it rest. Let it heal. Alone,
I remembered this little herb, the yellow spikes
of the flower, frill of stamen, as something akin
to happiness – its bright stars, its tiny play
at hope, its way of lifting through the grass –
and I brought it to you, a light to illumine
the dark caves of your eyes. At the door
of the ward, being searched, the nurse
took from me my gathering of flowers.
I found you on the bed, staring, still in shock.
Bringing no gift, I took your head
in my empty hands like a world and held it.

MARY O'MALLEY

The Heart Man

It is somewhere to the left
of centre. When he is asked
to picture it, he sees a dark space

a metal wrapping locked tight
to protect it from the touch of ravens
and whatever else is in there.

A shaman wants to flood it
with love, the healing breath,
lay all that raw flesh exposed

to his inner eye, pulsing red light.
The shaman tries and the casing creaks
in the man's chest. He is tired.

Next day, he wakes, decided.
"I will find my heart," he says,
"and breathe on it

like an injured bird now that I know
where it is. I'll clean out the rust
myself and see what happens next."

When he got it tuned he went to the pub
twice a week to hear music
that lifts the heart and makes time fly.

He was dancing with Madame Bonaparte
when it cut out. He folded so quietly that
the music played on, nice and stately.

MOYA CANNON

Sympathetic Vibration

For Kathleen

"You never strike a note,
You always take the note."

Did it take her many
of her eighty quiet passionate years
to earn that knowledge,
or was it given.

Music, the dark tender secret of it,
is locked into the wood of every tree.
Yearly, it betrays its presence
in minute fistfuls of uncrumpling green.

No stroke or blade can release the music
which is salve to ease the world's wounds,
which tells and, modulating, retells
the story of our own groping roots,
of the deep sky from which they retreat
and, in retreating, reach –
the tree's great symphony of leaf.

No stroke or blade can bring us that release
but sometimes, where wildness has not yet been stilled,
hands, informed by years of patient love,
can come to know the hidden rhythms of the wood,

can touch bow to gut
and take the note,
as the heart yields and yields
and sings.

RITA DOVE

The Secret Garden

I was ill, lying on my bed of old papers,
when you came with white rabbits in your arms;
and the doves scattered upwards, flying to mothers,
and the snails sighed under their baggage of stone ...

Now your tongue grows like celery between us:
Because of our love-cries, cabbage darkens in its nest;
the cauliflower thinks of her pale, plump children
and turns greenish-white in a light like the ocean's.

I was sick, fainting in the smell of teabags,
when you came with tomatoes, a good poetry.
I am being wooed. I am being conquered
by a cliff of limestone that leaves chalk on my breasts.

TOM FRENCH

After Adomnán

Because it seemed to sense that death was near
when it saw the old man pausing to rest
on the path where it had drawn milk to the monks,
like a person the horse began to mourn,

placing its head against its master's chest
until the old saint and his robe were drenched,
and servants intervened and did their best
to lead the creature back into the field.

But the saint implored that it not be touched –
"Those who have loved us and whom we have loved
must be permitted, at the very least,
to show each other what this life has meant."

Thus, the old man whose last day was at hand
held, until it had grieved its last, his friend.

Acknowledgements

'X-ray' by **Dannie Abse**, from *Ask The Moon* (Hutchinson, 2014), with kind
permission of the publisher. Copyright © Dannie Abse 2014. Reprinted by
permission of The Random House Group Limited.

'A Mother Mourns Her Heroin-Addicted Daughter' by **Leland Bardwell**,
from *The Noise of Masonry Settling* (Dedalus Press, 2006), with kind
permission of the publisher.

'Restriction' by **Tara Bergin**, from *This Is Yarrow* (Carcanet Press, 2013),
with kind permission of the author and publisher.

'The Man-Moth' by **Elizabeth Bishop**, from *POEMS* (Farrar, Straus and
Giroux, 2011). Copyright © 2011 by The Alice H. Methfessel Trust.
Publisher's Note and compilation copyright © 2011 by Farrar, Straus and
Giroux. Reprinted by permission of Farrar, Straus and Giroux. All Rights
Reserved.

'Quarantine' by **Eavan Boland**, from *New Collected Poems* (Carcanet Press,
2005), with kind permission of the publisher.

'The Nurse' by **Pat Boran**, from *The Next Life* (Dedalus Press, 2012), with
kind permission of the author and publisher.

'Infertility' by **Zoë Brigley**, from *Hand & Skull* (Bloodaxe Books, 2019),
with kind permission of the author and publisher.

'Old Lady' by **Christy Brown**, from *Of Snails and Skylarks* (Martin Secker &
Warburg, 1977). Copyright © 1977 Christy Brown. Reprinted by permission
of The Random House Group Limited.

'To Dr. Maxwell, On Miss Jessy Staig's Recovery' by **Robert Burns**, from
The Complete Poems and Songs of Robert Burns (Lomond Books, 2000).

'Doctor Verse' by **Siobhán Campbell**, from *The Cold that Burns* (Blackstaff
Press, 2000), with kind permission of the author.

'Sympathetic Vibration' by **Moya Cannon**, from *Oar* (Salmon Poetry, 1990),
with kind permission of the author and Carcanet Press.

'What the Doctor Said' by **Raymond Carver**, from *All of Us: The Collected
Poems* (Harvill Press, 1997). Copyright © Tess Gallagher 1996. Reprinted by
permission of The Random House Group Limited.

'Metastasis' by **Jane Clarke**, from *When the Tree Falls* (Bloodaxe Books,
2019), with kind permission of the author and publisher.

'A Son! A Son!' by **Harry Clifton**, from *The Winter Sleep of Captain Lemass*
(Bloodaxe Books, 2012), with kind permission of the author and publisher.

'Cross-Section with Contrast' by **Stephanie Conn**, from *Off-Kilter* (Doire
Press, 2022), with kind permission of the author and publisher.

'An archive' by **Hannah Copley**, from *Speculum* (Broken Sleep Books, 2021),
with kind permission of the author and publisher.

'A History of Snow' by **Paula Cunningham**, from *Queering the Green: Post-
2000 Queer Irish Poetry* (The Lifeboat Press, 2021), with kind permission of
the author and publisher.

'Alzheimer's' by **Pádraig J. Daly**, from *Clinging to the Myth* (Dedalus Press,
2007), with kind permission of the author and publisher.

'Going Under' by **Gerald Dawe**, from *Heart of Hearts* (The Gallery Press, 1995), with kind permission of the author and publisher.

'Chalice of My Blood' by **Celia De Fréine**, from *Blood Debts* (Scotus Press, 2014), with kind permission of the author and publisher.

'Cailís Mo Chuid Fola' by **Celia De Fréine**, from *Fiacha Fola* (Cló Iar-Chonnacht, 2004), with kind permission of the author and publisher.

'The Bullfield' by **Eoin Devereux**, with kind permission of the author.

'Crab-Apples' by **Imtiaz Dharker**, from *I Speak for the Devil* (Bloodaxe Books, 2001), with kind permission of the author and publisher.

'The Hospital Window' by **James Dickey**, from *The Whole Motion: Collected Poems 1945-1992* (Wesleyan University Press, 1994), with kind permission of the publisher.

'Surgeons Must Be Very Careful' by **Emily Dickinson**, from *The Collected Poems of Emily Dickinson* (Barnes and Noble Books, 1993).

'Anniversary: To a Father' by **Gerard Donovan**, from *The Lighthouse* (Salmon Poetry, 2000), with kind permission of the author and publisher.

'Skull of a Curlew' by **Theo Dorgan**, from *What This Earth Cost Us* (Dedalus Press, 2008), with kind permission of the author and publisher.

'The Secret Garden' by **Rita Dove**, from *Collected Poems* (W.W. Norton & Co., 2016), with kind permission of the author and publisher.

'The Touch' by **Tom Duddy**, with kind permission of Sheila Duddy.

'The Head Transplant' by **Paul Durcan**, from *Life Is A Dream: 40 Years Reading Poems: 1967-2007* (Harvill Secker, 2009). Reproduced by permission of the author c/o Rogers, Coleridge & White Ltd., 20 Powis Mews, London W11 1JN.

'The Moon is a Healing Being' by **Chiamaka Enyi-Amadi**, from *Winter Papers Volume 6* (Curlew Editions, 2020), with kind permission of the author and publisher.

'Flowers in the Attic' by **Martina Evans**, from *The Windows of Graceland* (Carcanet Press, 2016), with kind permission of the author and publisher.

'Egg' by **Elaine Feeney**, from *Rise* (Salmon Poetry, 2017), with kind permission of the author and publisher.

'Rainbow Blood' by **FELISPEAKS**, with kind permission of the author.

'Limbo' by **Cian Ferriter**, from *Earth's Black Chute* (Southword Editions, 2022), with kind permission of the author and publisher.

'Take it from the Spleen, Baby Doll' by **Órfhlaith Foyle**, from *Red Riding Hood's Dilemma* (Arlen House, 2010), with kind permission of the author and publisher.

'After Adomnán' by **Tom French**, from *The Sea Field* (The Gallery Press, 2020), with kind permission of the author and publisher.

'Menopause' by **Pamela Gillilan**, from *All-Steel Traveller* (Bloodaxe Books, 1994), with kind permission of the publisher.

'Returning from Illness' by **Vona Groarke**, from *Link: Poet and World* (The Gallery Press, 2021), with kind permission of the author and publisher.

'Diet' by **Victoria Kennefick**, from *Eat or We Both Starve* (Carcanet Press, 2021), with kind permission of the author and publisher.

'Top Surgery' by **William Keohane**, from *Poetry Ireland Review* 134, with kind permission of the author and Poetry Ireland.

'Treasure island' by **Aoife Lyall**, from *Mother, Nature* (Bloodaxe Books, 2021), with kind permission of the author and publisher.

'Athoscailt' / 'Reopening' by **Aifric Mac Aodha**, translated by **David Wheatley**, from *Poems from Pandemia* (Southword Editions, 2020), with kind permission of the author and publisher.

'Stop and Love the People' by **Paul McCarrick**, with kind permission of the author.

'The Argument for Chemotherapy' by **Shirley McClure**, from *Origami Doll: New and Collected Poems* (Arlen House, 2019), with kind permission of the publisher.

'Octopus' by **Gail McConnell**, from *Fourteen* (Green Bottle Press, 2018), with kind permission of the author.

'In The End ...' by **Terry McDonagh**, from *Ripple Effect* (Arlen House, 2013), with kind permission of the author and publisher.

'My Grandfather Battles Death' by **Karen J. McDonnell**, from *This Little World* (Doire Press, 2017), with kind permission of the author and publisher.

'Everything Is Going to Be All Right' by **Derek Mahon**, from *New Selected Poems* (The Gallery Press, 2016), with kind permission of the publisher.

'One Evening in May' by **Paula Meehan**, from *Pillow Talk* (The Gallery Press, 1994), with kind permission of the author.

'Leaving the Hospital' by **Wayne Miller**, from *Post-* (Milkweed Editions, 2016). Reprinted with the permission of The Permissions Company, LLC on behalf of Milkweed Editions.

'Cephalalgia' by **Geraldine Mitchell**, from *Mountains for Breakfast* (Arlen House, 2017), with kind permission of the author and publisher.

'& Forgive Us Our Trespasses' by **Sinéad Morrissey**, from *Between Here and There* (Carcanet Press, 2002), with kind permission of the author and publisher.

'The Field Hospital' by **Paul Muldoon**, from *Selected Poems*, (Faber and Faber Ltd., 1986), with kind permission of the author and publisher.

'Sirens' by **Emma Must**, from *Rear-View Mirror* (Poetry Ireland, 2017), with kind permission of the author and publisher.

'Scamhóga Áille' / 'Pink Lungs' by **Nuala Ní Chonchúir**, from *Tattoo: Tatú* (Arlen House, 2007), with kind permission of the author and publisher.

'The Polio Epidemic' by **Eiléan Ní Chuilleanáin**, from *Collected Poems* (The Gallery Press, 2020), with kind permission of the author and publisher.

'Bog Medicine' by **Annemarie Ní Churreáin**, from *Bloodroot* (Doire Press, 2017), with kind permission of the author and publisher.

'An Mhurúch san Ospidéal' / 'The Mermaid in the Hospital' by **Nuala Ní Dhomhnaill**, translated by **Paul Muldoon**, from *The Multilingual Mermaid* (The Gallery Press, 2021), with kind permission of the author and publisher.

'Cuair' / 'Curves' by **Áine Ní Ghlinn**, from *Gairdín Pharthais agus Dánta Eile* (Coiscéim, 1988), with kind permission of the author and publisher.

'Inventory: Recovery Room' by **Doireann Ní Ghríofa**, from *Clasp* (Dedalus Press, 2015), with kind permission of the author and publisher.

'Mumps' by **Nick Norwood**, with kind permission of the author.

'Holding Joe' by **James O'Leary**, from *There are Monsters in this House* (Southword Editions, 2018), with kind permission of the author and publisher.

'The Cure' by **Jean O'Brien**, from *Fish On A Bicycle* (Salmon Poetry, 2016), with kind permission of the author and publisher.

'Cleanse' by **Kerrie O'Brien**, with kind permission of the author.

Excerpt from 'Sketches for an Elegy' by **Julie O'Callaghan**, from *No Can Do* (Bloodaxe Books, 2000), with kind permission of the author and publisher.

'Doctors, Daughters' by **Mary O'Donnell**, from *The Place of Miracles* (New Island, 2006), with kind permission of the author and publisher.

'Ter Conatus' by **Bernard O'Donoghue**, from *Selected Poems* (Faber and Faber Ltd., 2008), with kind permission of the author.

'Admissions' by **Dennis O'Driscoll**, from *Collected Poems* (Carcanet Press, 2017), with kind permission of the publisher.

'The Heart Man' by **Mary O'Malley**, from *Gaudent Angeli* (Carcanet Press, 2019), with kind permission of the author and publisher.

'X-ray' by **Caitríona O'Reilly**, from *The Sea Cabinet* (Bloodaxe Books, 2006), with kind permission of the author and publisher.

'Fiabhras' / 'Fever' by **Seán Ó Ríordáin**, translated by **Greg Delanty**, from *Apathy is Out / Ní Ceadmhach Neamhshuim* (Bloodaxe / Cló Iar-Chonnacht, 2021), with kind permission of Cló Iar-Chonnacht.

'McQuade' by **Frank Ormsby**, from *A Store of Candles* (The Gallery Press, 1986), with kind permission of the author and Bloodaxe Books.

'Lightning' by **Leanne O'Sullivan**, from *A Quarter of an Hour* (Bloodaxe Books, 2018), with kind permission of the author and publisher.

'Haiku' by **Maeve O'Sullivan**, from *Initial Response* (Alba Publishing, 2011), with kind permission of the author.

'Mental Cases' by **Wilfred Owen**, from *The Complete Poems and Fragments* (Chatto and Windus, 1993).

'The Bees Have Been Cancelled' by **Maya C. Popa**, from *American Faith* (Sarabande Books, 2019). Reprinted with the permission of The Permissions Company, LLC on behalf of Sarabande Books.

'The Cranium' by **Maurice Riordan**, from *The Water Stealer* (Faber and Faber Ltd., 2013), with kind permission of the author and publisher.

'Colonoscope' by **Mark Roper**, from *Even So: New & Selected Poems* (Dedalus Press, 2008), with kind permission of the author and publisher.

'Brighid's Eve, Intensive Care' by **Breda Wall Ryan**, from *In A Hare's Eye* (Doire Press, 2015), with kind permission of the author and publisher.

'For My Father' by **Seni Seneviratne**, from *Unknown Soldier* (Peepal Tree Press, 2019), with kind permission of the author and publisher.

Special thanks to Rosie Lavan, Kerrie O'Brien,
Paul Lenehan, Molly O'Toole, Eoin Rogers,
Elizabeth Mohen, Anne Hendrick, Aifric Mac Aodha,
Muiris Houston, Aileen Patterson, Alan Hayes,
Máirín Nic Eoin, Caoimhín Mac Giolla Léith,
Ronan Kavanagh, Peggy Hughes,
Victoria Maitland, Ciara Breathnach.

For their philanthropic support, warm thanks are due to
Luke O'Neill and Thomas Dillon Redshaw.

Particular thanks also to former Directors of Poetry
Ireland, Maureen Kennelly and Niamh O'Donnell,
and current Director Liz Kelly, whose talents and
energies were central to the inception and
development of *Vital Signs*.

Martin Dyar grew up in Swinford, County Mayo. His first book of poems, *Maiden Names* (Arlen House), was shortlisted for the Pigott Poetry Prize. A recipient of the Patrick Kavanagh Poetry Award, he has written a play, *Tom Loves a Lord*, about the life of the poet Thomas Moore, and, in collaboration with the composer Ryan Molloy, a song cycle titled *Buaine na Gaoithe*. He has held creative writing fellowships at the University of Iowa and at the University of Limerick. He teaches in the School of Medicine at Trinity College Dublin.